Legacy

Legacy

Walter Chrysler Jr. and the Untold Story of Norfolk's Chrysler Museum of Art

Peggy Earle

UNIVERSITY OF VIRGINIA PRESS

CHARLOTTESVILLE AND LONDON

University of Virginia Press
Printed in the United States of America on acid-free paper

First published 2008

1 3 5 7 9 8 6 4 2

Library of Congress Cataloging-in-Publication Data

Earle, Peggy, 1949–
   Legacy : Walter Chrysler Jr. and the untold story of Norfolk's
   Chrysler Museum of Art / Peggy Earle.
        p.   cm.
   Includes bibliographical references and index.
   ISBN 978-0-8139-2718-3 (cloth : alk. paper)
   1. Chrysler, Walter P. (Walter Percy), 1909–1988. 2. Art—
Collectors and collecting—United States—Biography.
   3. Chrysler Museum. I. Title.
   N5220.C49E23 2008
   709.2—dc22
   [B]
                                                          2008002959

CONTENTS

CONTENTS

Acknowledgments

Art and museums have always played significant roles in my life. As a native New Yorker and an aspiring artist, I invariably spent weekends gazing at masterpieces in the Brooklyn, Metropolitan, Modern, Guggenheim, or Whitney. So it was from the perspective of a confessed art snob that I came to Norfolk in 1977. From the first of countless visits to the Chrysler Museum, however, I was astounded by the superb quality of its contents. The breadth and taste of the paintings and sculptures were quantum leaps beyond what I'd seen at other museums in comparably sized cities. More than once, as I strolled through the galleries, I couldn't help wondering, "What's a fabulous museum like you doing in a place like this?"

Since the 1970s, Hampton Roads has developed significantly; it has become more sophisticated, attractive, and culturally rich. But many tourists and even residents may not know the story of one of the region's most important cultural assets, much less how it came to be called the Chrysler Museum. I feel fortunate to be able to tell that story.

As much as possible, I have relied on interviews and oral

histories as sources for this narrative. Family members of Walter and Jean Chrysler, their friends and acquaintances, as well as current and former museum staff members provided colorful and entertaining first-person accounts.

But oral history is, by its nature, subjective. In addition to offering varied, sometimes contradictory opinions about the principal players, many of whom are deceased, some of these accounts include factual disparities. Memories tend to be fuzzy, especially when people are reaching back decades. As much as possible, therefore, I have tried to either corroborate or correct the most contentious points. In some cases, and for a variety of reasons, it is impossible to document what really happened.

I do know what happened to me. In the course of my research, I spent scores of delightful hours talking to people who graciously invited me into their homes and shared their time and recollections. Through them, a picture came into focus of a fascinating, enigmatic, and controversial man who was obsessed with collecting the art of the ages so it could be shared with the general public—but also so that it might stand as a monument to his name. The experience has been an education and a great privilege.

Among the many people who helped with my research, I want to thank librarians Matthew Wiggins and Jerry Flanary at the Jean Outland Chrysler Library of the Chrysler Museum, but especially Laura Christiansen, who so tirelessly and cheerfully went out of her way to find photos and get information for me on many occasions. Thanks to Kathy Albers at the *Richmond Times-Dispatch* library, Sarah Hartwell at Dartmouth College's Rauner Special Collections library, and very special thanks to my former colleagues Ann Kinken Johnson, Maureen Watts, Kimberly Kent, and Jakon Hays at the *Virginian-Pilot* library. The *Virginian-Pilot* arts writer

Teresa Annas so generously shared her expertise and reference materials with me. Invaluable, too, were Stefan Beck at the *New Criterion* magazine; Peter Macara and Jim Zimmerman at the Provincetown Artists' Association; and Dick Barry and Debbie Meads of Landmark Communications.

Suggestions and leads to important sources came from so many people, including Jane Goldman, Meredith Misek, Jean Booton, Anna Henderson, and Meredith Heywood. Johanna Climenko, the *New York Times* food writer Alex Witchel, and, especially, Douglas Turnbaugh were all essential to my extraordinary interview with Dr. Marguerite Nichols.

For permitting me access to unpublished memoirs of deceased, crucial players in the museum's history, I'm very grateful to Fran Mason Irvin for her kind permission to quote so liberally from her father's manuscript, and to Mrs. Louise Martin for allowing me access to her husband's words.

Thank you to Frank B. Rhodes Jr., Walter Chrysler's grand-nephew, for sharing his treasure trove of family photos with me and helping me reach Jack Chrysler Jr.

Warm thanks to my first editor, Bill Ruehlmann, for his careful attention to my words, as well as for his own encouraging words; and to the good friends (and terrific writers) who took the time and trouble to read my first draft and offer invaluable advice, Laura LaFay and Keith Monroe. To Earl Swift, who edited both drafts, you are my hero. To Boyd Zenner at the University of Virginia Press, thank you for your enthusiasm about the book and for your guidance on the final version. And to Susan Brady, thanks for your meticulous copyediting and friendly e-mail messages.

To all the people quoted in the book, please know that it would not exist without you. For those who don't see their names in the text, it was only due to lack of space. You all were just as important to the final product: Martha Stokes,

Marty Murphy, Tim Morton, Rick Salzberg, Robert Wojtowicz, Sara Bearss, John Wykert, Robert Gingold, and Corinne Jones.

How can I thank Bill Hennessey and the Chrysler Museum board for giving me the opportunity to do this project? To be associated with an institution that has been such a constant source of pleasure during my years in Norfolk has been one of the highlights of my life.

I'm deeply grateful to my dear friends who bolstered my spirits over the past four years. Thanks so much to John Earle, who helped in countless ways, and to my son, Zev Deans, whose professed pride in his mother means the world. And to Walt Phillips, whose love and reassuring words have seen me through the last hectic phases of rewrites, thank you.

Finally, I dedicate this book to the beloved memory of my parents, who surrounded me with culture and infused in me a profound appreciation of art.

Legacy

1

ROSEBUD

Walter Percy Chrysler Jr. took his last breath on the evening of Saturday, September 17, 1988. The seventy-nine-year-old man's health had been worsening for a few months as advanced prostate cancer took its toll. In a private room at Sentara Norfolk General Hospital, Chrysler spent that afternoon receiving a few visitors, mostly friends he had made since moving to Norfolk seventeen years earlier. One, who had known him since the late 1950s, was summoned to his bedside from New York. A Manhattan art dealer, Jack Tanzer observed that the typically rotund Chrysler had become frail and thin and was in obvious pain. Despite that, Chrysler held Tanzer's hand during an hour-long conversation and was lucid and pleasant until the pain forced an end to the visit.[1]

Chrysler, who had always refused to talk about death, had spent the previous year matter-of-factly telling everyone good-bye. At the urging of those closest to him in Norfolk, he had agreed to draft a new will. Chrysler's existing will had been signed nine years earlier, when he named his wife, Jean Outland Chrysler, as the primary beneficiary. There had been little doubt in the local art community that Jean, who was twelve years her husband's junior, would survive him and bequeath the bulk of his estate, including everything in his art collection, to the Chrysler Museum in her hometown of Norfolk. If she were to predecease her husband, however, the 1979 will provided that the estate would then fall to Chrysler's nephew, who had no particular attachment to Norfolk or its museum. In 1982, Jean Chrysler died suddenly of a cerebral hemorrhage.

At stake were 751 art objects, including exhibited works still marked "on loan" to the museum—Old Master paintings by Lucas Cranach the Elder and Jacopo Pontormo; nineteenth-century works by Jean-Auguste-Dominique Ingres and Theodore Géricault; eighteenth-century pictures by Jean-Honoré Fragonard; and art glass by Louis Comfort Tiffany. In addition, there were two houses in Norfolk and an apartment in Manhattan and all of their contents, including decorative art and Art Deco and Art Nouveau furniture. There was also trust money amounting to about $3 million.

Now, in his final days, Chrysler seemed prepared to sign the new will that would transfer all the art, property, and money originally bequeathed to Jean directly to the Chrysler Museum. An appointment was made for the will's signing in the presence of Philip R. Trapani, Norfolk's city attorney at the time and one of the only lawyers Chrysler trusted. But due to a serious car accident involving Trapani's wife and Trapani's own hospitalization for acute appendicitis and peritonitis, the appointment was postponed.

Arthur Diamonstein, a close friend of Chrysler's and a museum trustee, knew that Chrysler was near death. He pleaded with Chrysler to sign the papers with another lawyer. Chrysler refused; only Trapani would do. Finally, to the relief of all concerned, Trapani was well enough to reschedule the signing of the will for September 19, six days after

Chrysler had been admitted to the hospital. It was two days too late, as it turned out.

Museum staff, as well as the larger Hampton Roads arts community, reacted with shocked disbelief when they realized that a mere forty-eight hours had separated them from the bounty they had assumed was theirs. Instead, Jack Forker Chrysler Jr., the forty-five-year-old owner of Chrysler Aviation in Van Nuys, California, inherited the lion's share of the art, the real estate and its contents, and money from several Chrysler family trusts.

The Chrysler Museum received seventeen important American and European paintings that had formerly been on loan, a $1.6-million endowment, and 76 percent of an estimated $5-million family trust fund. Publicly, the museum's leadership tried to look on the bright side, focusing on Chrysler's original gifts, as well as the paintings and money bequeathed in the executed will. They chalked Chrysler's not signing the revised will up to a case of rotten luck.

There were those, however, who thought luck had had little to do with it. Some, like Thomas H. Willcox Jr., a Norfolk lawyer and the museum board's president at the time of Chrysler's death, believed he had never intended to sign the new will. Instead, they assumed he simply had been playing another in a series of manipulative games, using his will as a "carrot" with the museum's administration and board. Walter Chrysler, said Harvey Zimand, the New York attorney who had helped draft other versions of Chrysler's wills, always did exactly as he wanted.[2]

There is no way to know what Chrysler intended. Although he was a larger-than-life public figure, he was also intensely private, even secretive. He was a man of extreme contradictions who could inspire admiration and loyal affection as well as deep-seated scorn and resentment. What was indisputable was that for the majority of his seventy-nine years, while he had attempted a variety of careers and lifestyles, wed two wives, and suffered more than his share of scandals, Walter Chrysler was steadily amassing an extraordinary art collection. Much of that collection is housed in the Chrysler Museum of Art in Norfolk, one of the brightest jewels in southeastern Virginia's crown. Its handsome Italianate building, set at the head of the Hague inlet of the Elizabeth River, shelters a comprehensive treasure trove of international art that astonishes even the most skeptical out-of-town critics and is a permanent source of pride for area residents.

But before 1971 there was no Chrysler Museum. On its site was the Norfolk Museum of Arts and Sciences. A respectable community establishment for a city of Norfolk's size, the museum that officially opened in 1933 contained some fine exhibits mixed into an uneven collection. A modest but active art school operated under the museum's auspices, as did displays of a variety of small animals, living and stuffed.

During World War II, when a young Norfolk gym teacher named Jean Outland met and married U.S. Navy Lieutenant Walter P. Chrysler Jr., the museum's eventual transformation was inadvertently set in motion. Chrysler, son and namesake of the legendary automobile magnate, had already accumulated a stellar collection of paintings, sculpture, and decorative art. In 1958, he installed the work in the Chrysler Museum of Art, which he founded in Provincetown, Massachusetts. Twelve years later, thanks to his wife's ties to the area and the vision of Norfolk's leaders, Chrysler was persuaded to select the Museum of Arts and Sciences as a new home for his collection.

As often occurs when significant change is proposed, some community members embraced the idea of the Chrysler Museum, while others fought it furiously. Nevertheless, Walter Chrysler and his art were there to stay. The museum's rebirth sparked a cultural chain reaction in Norfolk that included the founding of the Virginia Opera Association and the Virginia Stage Company. It changed the face of the city and attracted an unprecedented influx of industry and tourism to the entire region.

Walter P. Chrysler Jr. has been compared in the press to the protagonist in the classic film *Citizen Kane*. Like Charles Foster Kane, Chrysler accumulated an astronomical number of things, ranging in quality from masterpieces to downright schlock. He shopped every day until illness prevented him, filling his homes, museums, and warehouses with objects, as had Kane with his gaudy Xanadu. But unlike Orson Welles's cinematic protagonist, who died leaving nothing but an enigmatic last word—Rosebud—Walter Chrysler left an enduring legacy. He permanently transformed a small city museum into an internationally esteemed showplace. This is the story of how it happened.

2

THE NORFOLK MUSEUM OF ARTS AND SCIENCES

In 1871, exactly a century before the founding of the Chrysler Museum, Irene Kirke Leache and Anna Cogswell Wood established a school in Norfolk for well-to-do young women. The Leache-Wood Seminary offered a liberal arts education and served as a counterpart to the all-male Norfolk Academy. When Leache died in 1900, Wood and some former students created the Irene Leache Library Association, which sponsored lectures and concerts and exhibited donated artworks along with the pieces the two women had brought back from their travels in Europe. Before 1902, when she left Norfolk for a long residence in Italy, Wood was instrumental in the formation of the Leache-Wood Alumnae Association. When World War I forced her return to Norfolk in 1914, Wood combined the library and alumnae associations into the Irene Leache Art Association, a group dedicated to promoting the arts with a long-range goal of creating a museum.

The Leache Association's small art collection, housed temporarily at the Norfolk Public Library's Freemason Street building, consisted mostly of reproductions and decorative items. It was, nevertheless, the closest thing to a museum the city had ever seen, and as such, was a cultural benchmark.[1] Over the next two years, the Leache Association offered prizes for original work in art, poetry, music, and drama, as well as hosting lectures and becoming part of a national arts group. In 1915, Douglas Volk, an artist lecturing there, suggested a less provincial name for the growing organization. As the Norfolk Society of Arts, with the Irene Leache Library (later, the Irene Leache Memorial) serving as its cultural arm, the group opened its membership to the community in 1917.[2]

One of the new members of the society was Florence Sloane, whose husband, William, had made his fortune in textiles. Their Tudor-style home on Norfolk's Lafayette River would later become known as the Hermitage Foundation Museum. Florence Sloane offered the society land, at Mowbray Arch and Fairfax Avenue, and later financed construction of a building on it to temporarily house the group's art collection.[3]

In 1928, Sloane chaired the building committee for a permanent structure, to which she contributed proceeds of the sale of the Fairfax Avenue house. The first wing of the Norfolk museum, which would eventually become the Chrysler, was erected at the head of the Hague inlet on land donated by the city.

On February 28, 1933, with music provided by the Maury High School orchestra, a preview of the finished museum was held for more than a thousand area schoolchildren. Girl Scouts guided the children through the building they had helped finance with their donated pennies.[4] Then, on March 5—one day after Franklin Delano Roosevelt took the oath of the presidency with the promise of a "New Deal" to Depression-weary America—the Norfolk Museum of Arts and Sciences formally opened its doors to the public. The museum's inaugural exhibit consisted of European works of decorative and fine art, on loan from other museums.

For the first twelve years of the Norfolk Museum's existence, Florence Sloane served, without pay, as the museum's director. The all-volunteer staff was eventually replaced with one paid by the City of Norfolk. A 1938 government grant covered the building's first expansion.[5] Over the years, the museum hosted American literati like Robert Frost, who read his poetry there. In 1948, the Norfolk Museum was one of only five in the country to host a traveling show of 135 Parisian contemporary paintings, including works by Picasso, Bonnard, Matisse, Dufy, Laurencin, and Villon.

The permanent art collection continued to grow thanks to individual gifts and corporate donations. In addition, the museum's science section expanded with the opening of the Tidewater Natural History Division. Exhibits there featured animals preserved through taxidermy—screech owls, flying squirrels, snakes, and the like.

Robert H. Mason, a former editor of the *Virginian-Pilot,* was a trustee of both the Norfolk Museum and the Chrysler for eighteen years. In his unpublished manuscript "In Museumland," Mason related, with humor spiced with stinging social critique, some of his experiences on the museum boards. Mason took particular aim at one major player in the controversy surrounding the conversion of the Norfolk Museum of Arts and Sciences to the Chrysler Museum, a lawyer named William L. Parker, who was known by the childhood nickname "Judge" and was president of the Norfolk Museum's board of trustees for eighteen years until he resigned in 1971:

> Judge Parker declared the museum to be, public building and funding and mayoral influence notwith-

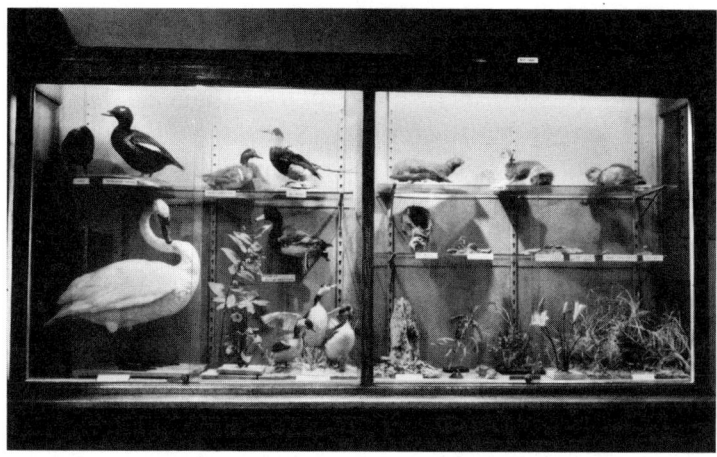

Stuffed wildlife on display in the science section of the Norfolk Museum of Arts and Sciences, 1959. (Courtesy of the Chrysler Museum of Art, Norfolk, Va.; photograph by Photocraftsmen, Inc.)

standing, a private organization entitled to say who could be, for a $10 fee earmarked for acquisitions, a member—"just as private," he told a newspaper reporter, "as the German Club," which held dominion over the yearly crop of Norfolk debutantes. The museum membership was as lily-white as the debs.

From the hour of Jim Crow's demise back in 1960, the Norfolk Museum of Arts and Sciences never lacked for fuss. A nature group protested when a room was cleared of stuffed wildlife, notably mean-looking cottonmouth moccasins snagged in the swamps by a part-time curator named Roger Rageot, to make way for a collection of Confederate Navy artifacts. The Junior League became upset when first a budgetary problem and then a personnel change threatened its docent program. The museum art school, waxing and waning, encouraged as much debate as talent.[6]

Throughout this period, gifts of great generosity were bestowed on the Norfolk Museum, including the monumental sculpture donated by the artist Anna Hyatt Huntington in 1957. Huntington's *The Torchbearers* is an eighteen-foot-high, three-thousand-pound cast-aluminum statue depicting a dying man handing a burning torch to another man on horseback. These dynamic figures still hold the place of honor in front of the entrance to the Chrysler Museum.

A gift of $500,000 was given to the Norfolk Museum upon the death of an anonymous donor in 1960. It was the largest single gift in the museum's history, and it went toward a matching fund set up by the city to be used for further expansion. A *Virginian-Pilot* editorial waxed lyrical about the museum at that time: "Built in the design of a Florentine palace, it stands as a symbol of that period known as the Italian Renaissance when there was a reawakening of men's minds and genius was nourished on every side by an uplifting of the human spirit after a long, dark period of thralldom. . . . Reflected in the mirror of The Hague, it is itself a work of art."[7]

The historic Selden House, on Botetourt Street in downtown Norfolk, was soon loaned to the museum for its educational headquarters. Classes on such crafts as ceramics, weaving, and bookbinding were offered. "The natural historian moved into the basement," recalled Matthew Werth, the museum's business manager from 1962 to 1971. "People would sometimes hang a live rattlesnake on the front door in a bag—you could hear it—for him to add to his collection. It was very colorful."[8]

Toward the end of 1963, the Norfolk Museum received two windfalls. Jean Outland Chrysler donated forty-two contemporary paintings, drawings, and sculptures to the museum in honor of her parents. The gift was lauded as one of the finest

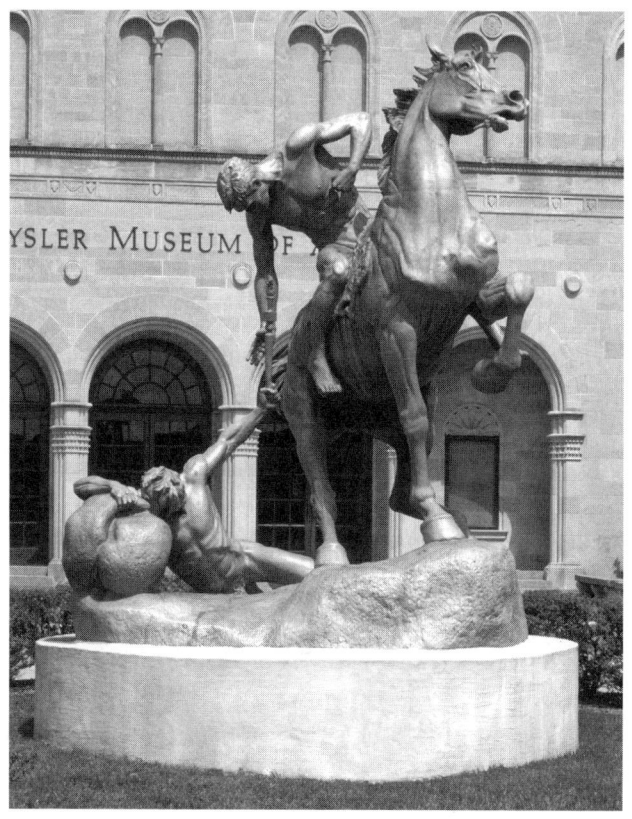

The Torchbearers, by Anna Hyatt Huntington, modeled 1953, cast 1956–57 (cast aluminum, 266 in.). This elegant grouping still graces the front entrance of the Chrysler Museum, facing an inlet known as the Hague. (Chrysler Museum of Art, Norfolk, Va., gift of the artist to the City of Norfolk. Photo courtesy of the Chrysler Museum of Art, Norfolk, Va., © Estate of Anna Hyatt Huntington.)

collections of American Abstract Expressionist art south of Washington, D.C. Another gift, the Alfred Khouri Memorial Collection, consisting of some 250 pictures and sculptures, arrived that year as well.

In the same year, the *Virginian-Pilot* reported that people were visiting the museum in increasing numbers: "They're coming to look at new pictures. They're coming to demonstrations and movies; they're coming to hear folk-singing and barbershop quartets." The writer also opined that the museum was no longer guilty of combining "the worst aspects of a cathedral and a country club."[9] Not remarked upon in the article was the fact that, while its galleries were open to the general public, the Norfolk Museum still maintained an unwritten policy of segregation with regard to its membership.

In 1964, the museum announced plans to build a $1.2-million wing that would double the building's current size. The $600,000 gift of Wilmer Willis Houston, a Norfolk businessman known for his wide-ranging civic generosity, had been matched by the city council. The proposed new wing was to be added to the east and south sides of the existing building and included a four- or five-story tower that would rise from where the two sections were joined. Also planned were a new sculpture garden, roughly twice as large as the existing courtyard garden, and an expanded natural history gallery to be presided over by Roger Rageot, who had come to Norfolk after a brief stint building natural history exhibits for the Smithsonian.

Later that year, a majority of board members at last voted to integrate the museum's membership. Judge Parker announced the names of four new African American members, including A. B. Jackson, a talented artist who had received both undergraduate and master's degrees from Yale and who was chairman of the art department at Norfolk State College (now Norfolk State University).[10] Also around this time, the museum's education department, under Richard Carroll, got its first African American docent, Mrs. Corinne Jones.

By 1967, museum director Henry Bryan Caldwell had accomplished a great deal. On his watch, membership and attendance had increased; the docent program, staffed primarily by Junior League volunteers, had grown; the art school at the Selden House had been established; a rent-to-own art service was initiated; local and regional artists were supported by juried shows and regular exhibits; and the science program was expanding.

But two areas of vital concern for the museum remained: its lack of money and prestige. The Virginia Museum in Richmond was a significant obstacle in funding for its Norfolk counterpart. As the "official" state art museum, the Virginia Museum was well-supported by lawmakers. Norfolk's depended solely upon local tax income that barely covered the expenses of maintenance and salaries.

As for the Norfolk Museum's prestige, its small, worthy permanent collection needed enhancing. Fund-raisers like the popular "Festival in Florence," in which a footbridge near the museum was transformed into a miniature Ponte Vecchio from which merchants hawked their wares, couldn't come close to raising the sort of money necessary to purchase a good Cezanne, not to mention an Old Master. Without a curatorial staff, the museum lacked professional authority, while having works displayed that had questionable attribution naturally detracted from the institution's authenticated objects.[11]

On November 29, 1967, the Norfolk Museum's new Willis Houston Memorial Wing was dedicated, and one of the special events to celebrate its opening was a loaned exhibit titled Italian Renaissance and Baroque Painting from the

Collection of Walter P. Chrysler Jr. The show, consisting of seventy-five works by Italian artists of the fourteenth and fifteenth centuries, was pronounced one of the finest privately mounted outside Italy.[12] In March 1968, the Children's Natural History wing opened. It featured permanent displays of caged live animals, including an armadillo, as well as flora- and fauna-related artwork.

A few months later, a dispute arose over control of the Norfolk Museum of Arts and Science's board of trustees. The city council held back an appropriation of almost $100,000 because the board, represented by Judge Parker, refused to allow the council to appoint six trustees instead of three. City Manager Thomas F. Maxwell told Parker that the request for more city representation on the board came from Assistant City Attorney Philip R. Trapani.[13] Trapani, who became city attorney in 1975, would prove to be a major player in the history of what would become the Chrysler Museum, both as museum counsel and as one of Walter Chrysler's most trusted friends.

In 1969, as a result of budgetary constraints, the Norfolk Museum of Arts and Sciences was forced to eliminate its live animal exhibits and let the caged creatures return to the wild. A short time later, the executive board agreed to a compromise: they would keep a portion of the natural history exhibits on display but dismiss the program's director, whose office was to be converted into a library and board room. At about the same time, the city council unanimously appointed Walter P. Chrysler Jr. to the museum's board of trustees. Mayor Roy Martin proposed Chrysler's name to fill a vacancy left by the resignation of Norfolk businessman Henry Clay Hofheimer II the year before.

Judge Parker, delighted by the council's actions, cited Jean Chrysler's gifts as well as Walter Chrysler's loans as justification for the appointment. He lavished praise on Chrysler for his expertise in museum administration and talent for collecting fine art.[14] Parker's compliments were offered from a safe distance. Chrysler, at the time, seemed securely ensconced in his small museum in Provincetown and was, to most people in the Tidewater area, a beneficent abstraction with a famous last name. There was no way of knowing how Norfolk's museum community would be divided by the eccentric art collector who was born into one of New York's wealthiest and most famous families.

3

THE AUTO BARON'S SON

Walter Chrysler Jr. began life in extravagant wealth, the son of the visionary automobile tycoon who embodied the American self-made man. The elder Chrysler was born in 1875, one year before the massacre at Little Big Horn. Growing up in Ellis, Kansas, Walter Sr. heard enough tales of Indian attacks to terrify any little boy living in a frontier town. In his autobiography, Chrysler credited conquering those fears to the same strength and resilience that would later help him achieve his dreams.[1]

Having his own father, Henry (Hank) Chrysler, as a role model may have had something to do with it, too. When Hank—a Canadian of German stock whose family name had been changed from Greisler—was only twelve, he ran away from home, joined the Twelfth Kansas Regiment, and served as a Civil War drummer boy until the fighting ended. By the time Walter Sr. was born, his father was an engineer with the Union Pacific Railroad.[2]

Walter's dream was to be a railroad man, too. Against his father's wishes—Hank wanted a college education for his son—Walter finagled a job as a janitor in the machine shop

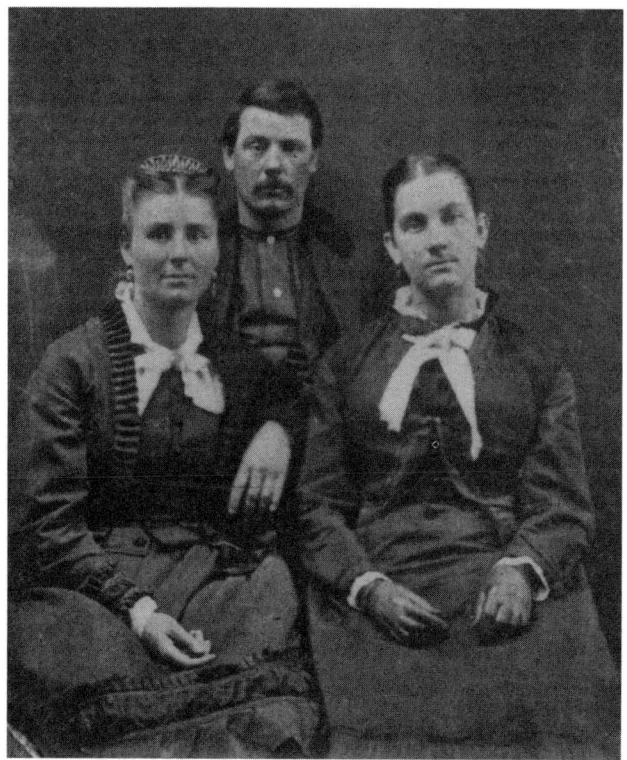

Walter Chrysler Jr.'s grandparents, Henry (Hank) Chrysler and Anna Maria Breyman, 1870. The woman on the right may be Anna's sister. (Courtesy of the Chrysler Museum of Art, Norfolk, Va.)

until Hank relented and allowed Walter to become an apprentice, earning five cents an hour. The younger Chrysler was a voracious learner, eager to understand every mechanical innovation, and when his apprenticeship ended, he hopped freight trains to wherever railroad jobs were offered.

By 1900, when he'd saved enough money, Walter Chrysler Sr. married his longtime sweetheart. Della Forker was a wealthy, exceptionally pretty, and talented young woman who played piano and could have had her pick of beaux in Ellis. But she must have seen potential in the ambitious railroad mechanic, and she proved to be his perfect mate, providing her husband with a seemingly endless supply of patience and support. The couple's first child, Thelma, was born two years later. Chrysler continued to travel with his growing family—a second daughter, Bernice, was born in 1906—advancing professionally and proving to be a great financial and organizational asset wherever he worked.

In 1908, Chrysler went to Chicago to attend the city's eighth annual automobile exposition. He was so excited by what he saw there that he borrowed nearly five thousand dollars to buy a new Locomobile touring car. Della, with two children already and another on the way, never impeded her husband's actions, even when they sank the family into debt. Before even learning to drive the newfangled vehicle, Chrysler had taken it apart and reassembled it several times.

The family was living in Oelwein, Iowa, when, on May 27, 1909, Walter Percy Chrysler Jr. was born. Oddly, in his autobiography, Chrysler Sr. devotes barely a sentence to the arrival of his first son.[3] More moves followed: to Pittsburgh, where a second son, John—better known as Jack—arrived in 1912, and then on to Flint, Michigan, where Chrysler, recognizing the potential of the auto industry, took a 50 percent cut in pay to work at the Buick Motor Company. Before long, he had reduced costs at Buick and increased its production of cars by doing away with waste and improving the assembly line.

After three years at Buick, Chrysler demanded and received a significant pay raise. He began to buy stock in Buick's parent company, General Motors. In 1916, he became the general manager of Buick and later, its president.

By now, Chrysler's salary was up to $500,000 a year, mostly in GM stock. He became unhappy with the company's business strategy, however, and at age forty-five, he quit GM, sold his stock, and retired.

Della Chrysler soon wearied of her husband and his friends constantly hanging around the house, filling it with noisy chatter and tobacco smoke. Luckily, when she urged Chrysler to return to work, he was ready to go.[4] In 1920, he was offered the vice presidency of the Willys-Overland Company. John Willys promised Chrysler $1 million a year if he could turn the foundering business around; within months, Chrysler had dramatically reduced the company's enormous debt. During this period, Chrysler began making plans to produce his own car.

In 1924, the first Chrysler automobile was introduced to the market. By the following year, Chrysler had earned $50 million in sales of his car, absorbed the Maxwell and Chalmers companies, and acquired Dodge Motor Company's plants. By 1929, the Chrysler Corporation joined Ford and General Motors to comprise the three largest auto manufacturers in the country; five years later, the company had mushroomed into the second-largest auto producer in the world.

The Chryslers were living luxuriously in Manhattan when, in 1923, Chrysler bought an immense, elegant estate from Henri Bendel, a New York designer and retail fashion millionaire. The summer home, at King's Point near Great Neck, Long Island, is now the site of the U.S. Merchant Marine Academy. It fronts 450 feet on a part of Long Island Sound dubbed the "Gold Coast" and immortalized in F. Scott Fitzgerald's *The Great Gatsby*. The house had twenty-three rooms, including a chapel, an indoor swimming pool, a gymnasium, and a billiards room. Twelve acres of grounds

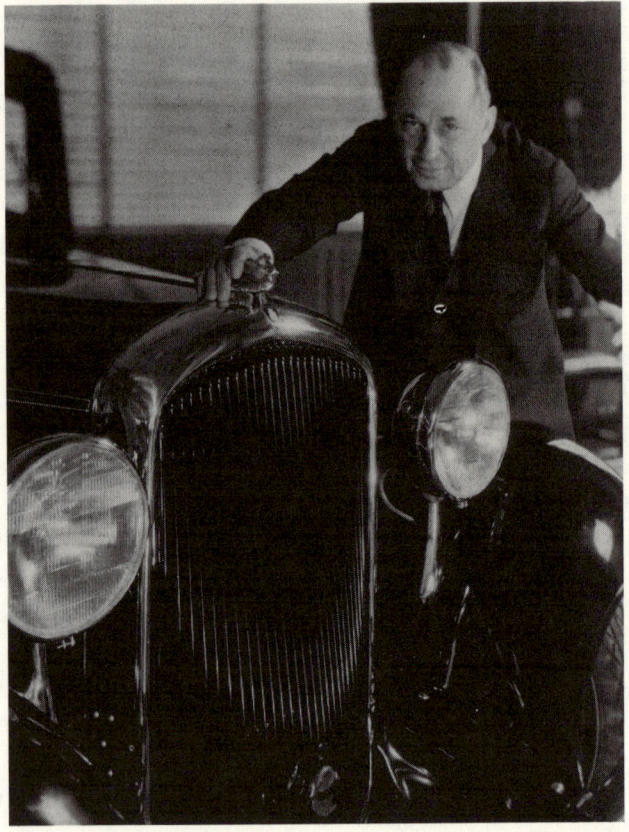

Walter Percy Chrysler Sr., March 29, 1932. (Courtesy of the Chrysler Museum of Art, Norfolk, Va.; photograph by Lee Anderson Advertising Agency.)

contained an enormous outdoor pool, a pier, and a boat-house.[5]

It was at King's Point and in a Park Avenue apartment that Walter Chrysler Jr. spent his early years. From the start, one of his favorite pastimes was collecting things. First came mechanical banks, a hobby in which his father joined. The two eventually accumulated one of the largest collections of

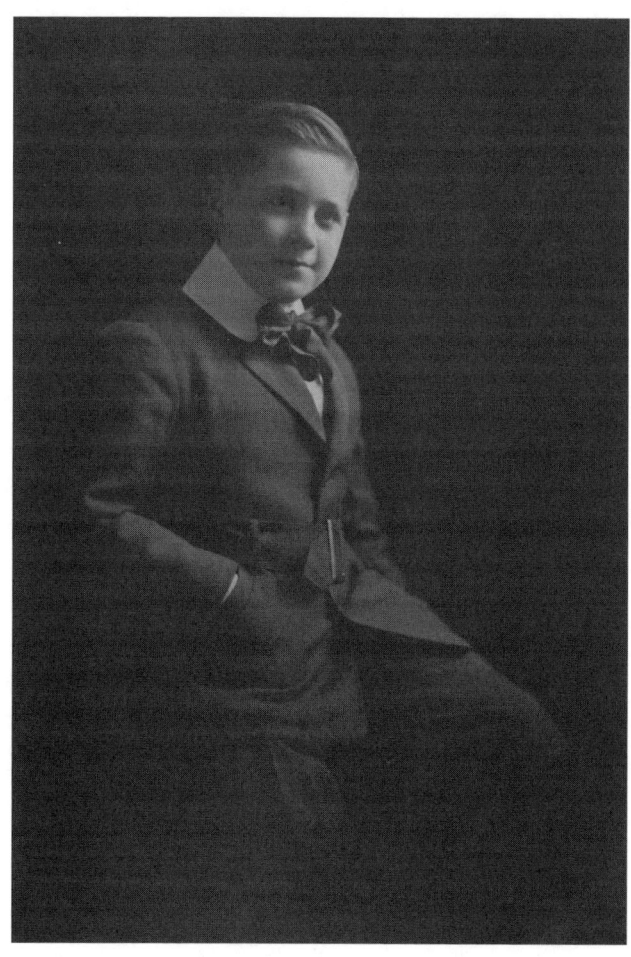

Walter Chrysler Jr. about eleven years old, in Flint, Michigan. (Courtesy of the Chrysler Museum of Art, Norfolk, Va.; photograph by Becker, Flint, Michigan.)

its type in the country. Encouraged by his maternal grandfather, Walter then began collecting stamps, and an uncle introduced him to numismatics, specifically American coins.[6]

The Chrysler family homes were filled with fine and decorative pieces, so it was perhaps inevitable that the young
stamp and coin collector would eventually turn to art objects, as well. The source of Walter's future obsession with
glass has been traced to his acquaintance with Louis Comfort Tiffany, whose Long Island summer home was located
near the Chryslers'. As an adult, however, Chrysler Jr. would
most often name his mother as the person who influenced
his future as an art maven. Della Chrysler saw to it that her
children were taken to museums and galleries on a regular
basis.

She was also credited as a pacifying influence on her husband's volatile temperament, a trait for which their first-born
son also would become well known.[7] The two Walters shared
other, more positive, qualities. They were both said to have
possessed an irresistible charm, and Walter Chrysler Jr.'s
compulsive attention to detail and penchant for microman-
aging practically every aspect of his businesses was surely
a version—albeit distorted—of his father's insistence on
learning a trade from the ground up.

As an adolescent, Walter was already showing an innate talent for recognizing and appreciating great art. On his fourteenth birthday, his father gave him the then-extravagant
sum of three hundred dollars to spend however he wished.
Walter bought a small Renoir watercolor of a landscape featuring a tiny figure of a nude woman.[8] He took the painting with him that year to Hotchkiss, a private boys' board-
ing school. Set amid the rolling foothills of the Connecticut
Berkshires, Hotchkiss was as conservative as it was exclusive.
When Walter's housemaster saw the Renoir on the dormitory
wall, he immediately pronounced it obscene and, depending

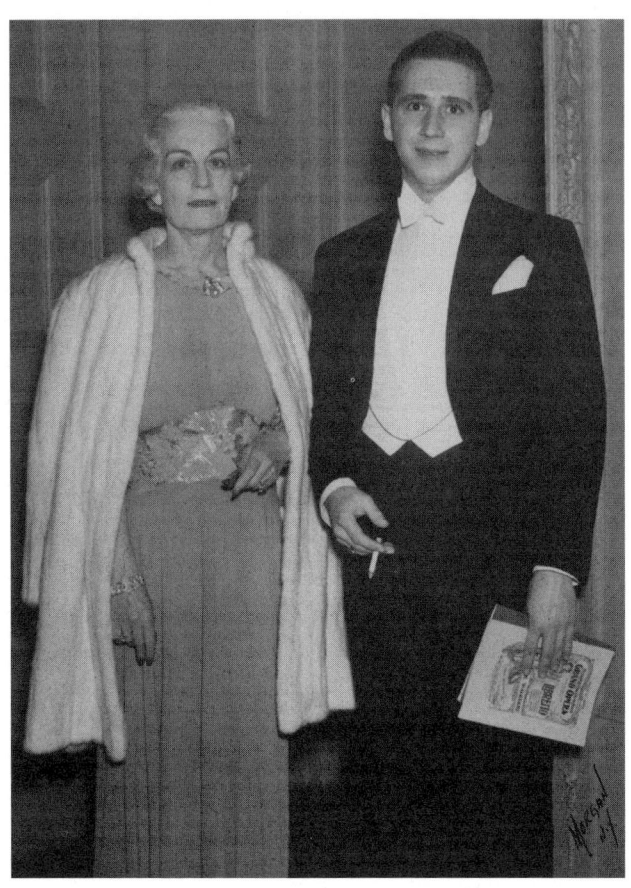

Della Viola Forker Chrysler and her son Walter P. Chrysler Jr.,
ca. 1930s. Walter credited his mother with instilling in him his life-
long interest in art. (Courtesy of the Chrysler Museum of Art, Norfolk, Va.; photograph by Morgan Photo Services, New York)

on which version of the much-repeated story was told, either tore it to pieces or cracked the framed picture across his knee.

Walter seemed out of step at Hotchkiss in other ways. While the teenager participated in the school's athletics—he was a member of the boxing team—he did not excel in any sport. He preferred editing the weekly school newsletter, in which he poked fun at the institution's rigid restrictions.[9]

When he was seventeen, Walter suffered the first in a life-long series of health problems, hemorrhaging so badly from bleeding ulcers that he had to be rushed to Manhattan by ambulance.[10] He recovered, was graduated, and set out on a round-the-world cruise with his mother and sister Bernice—a trip during which the Chryslers were entertained by international royalty, including the emperor of Japan.

On his return, Walter entered Dartmouth College, where, with fellow student Nelson Rockefeller (Walter Chrysler Sr. and John D. Rockefeller had long been friends), he sponsored and edited a bound magazine called the *Five Arts*. Walter was also active in the college's theater program and was able to bring New York speakers and exhibitions onto campus, as well as host soirées of music and poetry in his off-campus digs.[11]

In 1930, the Chrysler Building opened. In his autobiography, Walter Chrysler Sr. wrote that he built the Art Deco masterpiece as a labor of love for his four children.[12] The landmark skyscraper stands at the corner of Forty-second Street and Lexington Avenue and was, until the following year when the Empire State Building was completed, the tallest building in the world. The Chrysler Building, which housed the corporate headquarters for his company, also included a private apartment and office suite that Chrysler maintained on the top floor. The remaining offices were rented out.[13] He expected his first-born son to manage the seventy-seven-story tower and gave him express orders to acquaint himself with it by spending time in the basement, scrubbing floors, and cleaning offices. "He did it, too," Chrysler Sr. wrote, "and then proceeded through various jobs until he was well able to run the building."[14] Walter would serve on the skyscraper's board until it sold in 1953.

When he was twenty-one, Walter became the youngest publisher in the business when he founded Cheshire House, Inc. The company, with headquarters in the Chrysler Building, printed classics such as Dante's *Inferno* in leather-bound and illustrated collectible editions. His books garnered several awards from within the industry, but the venture failed commercially. In the early 1930s, with the country in the throes of the Depression, the time may not have been right to market such luxuries.

All the while, Walter Chrysler Jr. was distracted by what would become an abiding obsession: Art. He left Dartmouth after his junior year, in June 1931, and never graduated. Instead, he began making trips to Europe, where he bought modern art directly from masters including Picasso, Braque, Gris, Matisse, and Léger.[15]

In 1932, Walter opened his own art gallery. He named the gallery "The Cheshire," and housed it on the ground floor of the Chrysler Building. There, he told the *New York Times,* he planned to present works by international artists in various styles.[16] He later became involved with the fledgling Museum of Modern Art as the first chairman of its library committee. He helped build up the library's collection and, in 1936, donated the Paul Eluard-Camille Dausse collection of Surrealist materials.[17]

By then, the auto baron's "chunky, art-loving son"[18] had developed an interest in domestic air-conditioning. In 1934, he had become chairman and president of Temperature

Corp., a sales corporation that marketed an air-cooling, air-washing, dehumidifying device known as "Airtemp." By the 1940s, Airtemp would be the first air-conditioning system for use in vehicles, but it wasn't widely available for automobiles until the mid-1950s. A recent biography of Walter Chrysler Sr. casts doubt on the depth of his son's involvement in Airtemp, maintaining that the project was always under the senior Chrysler's control. Walter was probably just placating his father, Vincent Curcio wrote, after the falling out the two had the year before. Its cause was a book about a sensational rape/murder case that was to be published by Cheshire House. Chrysler loudly disapproved of the book's lurid subject matter; his son eventually gave in, the book was never printed, and Walter went to work for the Chrysler Corporation.[19] In 1935, he resigned from Temperature Corp. and became president of the W. P. Chrysler Building Corporation.

At that point, Walter was traveling to Europe on regular buying trips and gaining a reputation as a formidable collector. In a 1936 diary excerpt, the wife of Museum of Modern Art founder Alfred Barr mentions an incident in Paris in which Walter Chrysler Jr. was asked to help Barr purchase Picasso's *Three Musicians* for the museum. But Walter, wrote Margaret Scolari Barr, "in the midst of the complicated negotiations, flies back to the United States by zeppelin."[20]

Chrysler claimed to *Interview* magazine in 1978 that at one time he had more than 340 works by Picasso, but most were eventually traded so he could fill gaps in his increasingly diverse collection. To illustrate how canny he was when it came to art trading, which would later become his favored method of acquisition, Chrysler told *Interview* of a time in Paris when he and Gertrude Stein, the iconic American avant-garde writer and patroness of modern art, joined forces: "I remember there were two young men that she liked very much who wanted to set up in the gallery business. She said to me,

'Since you have a great collection, why don't you donate one of your pictures and I'll donate one of my pictures and that ought to put them in business. . . . I'll choose the picture from your collection and you choose the picture from my collection.' I forget now what picture she chose from my collection but I remember very well the picture I chose from her collection: Picasso's 'Two Women at the Bar.' I bought it from those boys as the first picture they sold, for $450. I later traded that for $1.6 million worth of pictures. So Gertrude Stein was very good for them and good to me."[21]

In a 1984 interview, Chrysler explained why, when possible, he purchased art directly from its source. "I prefer to see always from the artist's eye and heart—and to understand the work from that angle." He said he had to fall in love with everything he bought. "By the mid-30s," the reporter noted, "he was falling in love with a fervor that outstripped space to display his passions. Boxes and crates of art began to crowd his homes and his office in the Chrysler Building as the gourmand satisfied his desires."[22]

We'll never know what parts desire or love played in what followed, but in 1937 at a New York debutante ball, Walter Chrysler Jr. met a slender young woman who bore an almost uncanny resemblance to the young Bette Davis. At twenty-five, Marguerite Prince Sykes had acquired the sobriquet of "most sought-after girl in New York society."[23] The daughter of Walter H. Sykes Jr., a prominent New York Stock Exchange member who had died two years earlier, Marguerite (known as Peggy) became engaged to the auto baron's son in February 1938.

Decades later, Peggy Nichols—by then a doctor and widow of her second husband, Charles Nichols, a New York engineering executive and philanthropist—would recall meeting the Chrysler family early in her relationship with Walter.

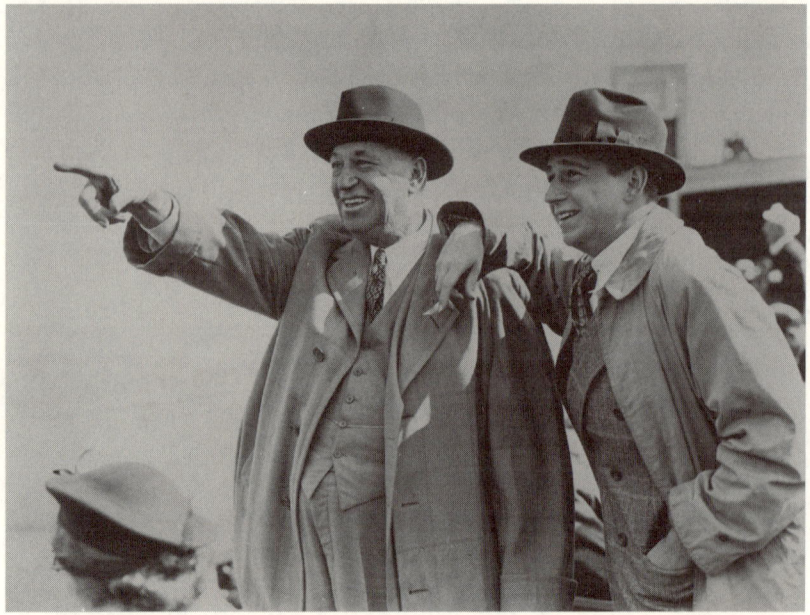

Walter Chrysler Sr. and his eldest son, Walter Chrysler Jr., ca. 1930s. (Courtesy of the Chrysler Museum of Art, Norfolk, Va.; photograph by De Lanos Studios, New York.)

She remembered being impressed by Della Chrysler's beauty and Chrysler Sr.'s sense of humor. Nichols said she got along particularly well with her future father-in-law and the feeling seemed mutual—especially when he observed how well the young woman took a rather cruel practical joke. On a visit to the Chryslers' home in Florida, while dressing for dinner, she washed her hands. Chrysler had left a bar of trick soap in her bathroom.[24]

"I looked at my hands and they were black," said Nichols. "So I washed them again and again, and they were still black! The gong kept ringing, and Mr. Chrysler was screaming, 'Miss Sykes, Miss Sykes, where are you?'"

Trying to keep her hands hidden, Nichols said, she sat

down next to the senior Chrysler. "He said, 'Anything wrong with your hands?' So I told him." When he admitted to having played the joke on her, the young woman joined him in laughter. "He was a remarkable man. I enjoyed him thoroughly.

"I think we were at a dinner party when Walter proposed," Nichols continued. "And I nodded to him. I came home and told my mother. I don't think she was terribly thrilled. I think she liked him, but she really didn't want to see me in that type of life." Nichols noted that while she shared a love of music with Chrysler, she never had any affection for his growing modern art collection.

On April 29, 1938, Walter P. Chrysler Jr. and Marguerite Prince Sykes married in Manhattan's St. Bartholomew's Church. Walter's brother, Jack, was best man. The ushers were his brothers-in-law, Byron C. Foy and Edgar W. Garbisch, and a close friend, Frank A. Vanderlip Jr. Among several wedding photos published in a *Life* magazine story was one of Walter's parents, at what turned out to be their last public event together. Wearing top hat and tails, Walter Chrysler Sr.'s head is thrown back in a jubilant laugh as Della smiles demurely. The accompanying article stressed the union of two elite families and mentioned the couple's upcoming five-month European honeymoon. Afterward, Walter and his new bride, photographed grinning broadly at each other, would settle into his fourteen-room Fifth Avenue apartment.[25]

"On our honeymoon, we went to Paris," Nichols recalled, "and he would say to me, 'Get dressed up and look poor.' I spoke beautiful French, and so I'd go off and I'd [bargain] down all these people for paintings for him. He bought a lot on our honeymoon. We met Picasso, and I know that one of my greatest mistakes was that he wanted to paint me and I said no. Can you imagine? I was out of my mind. I didn't want five noses and six eyes!" Nichols recalled Chrysler buying at

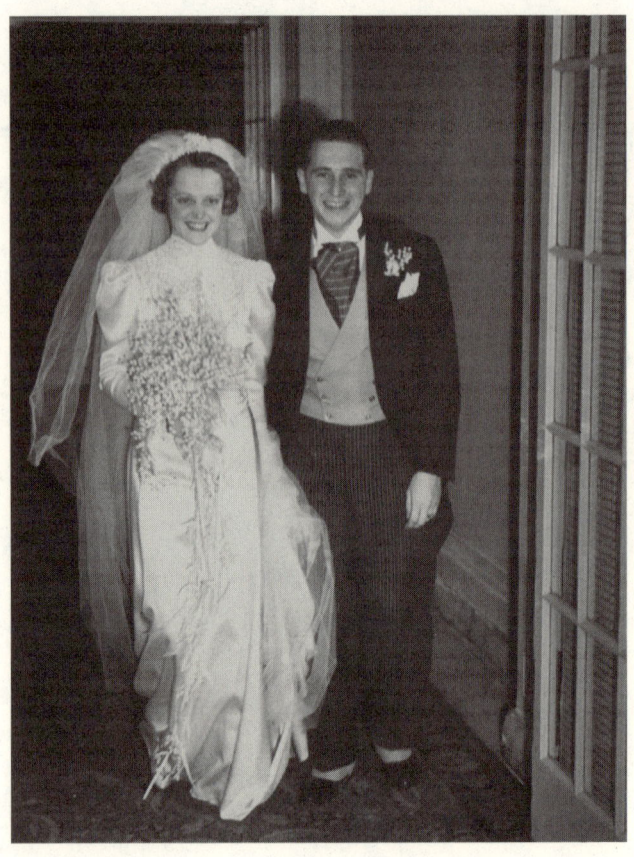

Walter and his first wife, Marguerite (Peggy) Sykes, on their wedding day, April 29, 1933, in New York City. The marriage lasted only slightly more than a year, possibly due to Walter's homosexuality. (Courtesy of the Chrysler Museum of Art, Norfolk, Va.; photograph by David Berns, New York.)

least ten large paintings by various artists during their honeymoon trip.

While the newlyweds were overseas, Chrysler Sr., aged sixty-three, suffered a stroke. He was hospitalized and released after several weeks. Then, during his recuperation at King's Point, came a much greater blow. Della Chrysler's health had become frail the year before as a result of complications following an appendectomy. Her husband's apparent brush with death took a further toll on her. On August 7, she complained of a headache and went to bed early. During the night, she lost consciousness, and, by seven o'clock the next evening, she was dead from a cerebral hemorrhage.[26] Walter and Peggy Chrysler cut their honeymoon short after Chrysler Sr.'s stroke, returning in time to join Walter's sister Thelma at their mother's bedside during her final hours.

The newlyweds soon settled into their homes in Manhattan and Great Neck. They enjoyed going to gala opera premieres and concerts together, but, Nichols said, "He was always off with art—that was his main interest." In their New York apartment, Peggy changed places with Walter at their dining room table so as not to sit opposite a large Picasso portrait of a woman. "I couldn't eat; it was the most disagreeable-looking painting I'd ever seen in my entire life." Another modern piece created a different sort of problem. At the end of the private road that led to the couple's summer house in Great Neck, Walter installed a recently purchased statue. "It was of a nude man and it was huge," said Nichols. "*Everything* on the man was double the size it should be!"

Nichols was referring to Gaston Lachaise's bronze *Man*, which now stands on the second floor of the Chrysler Museum in Norfolk. It was placed there after years outdoors, facing the relatively busy Olney Road, where it shocked some citizens and prompted complaints within the city council.

The statue's genitalia were even attacked by a hammer-wielding vandal. In Great Neck, said Peggy Nichols, "all of a sudden, there was so much traffic on the road. Everybody wanted to see it." When she offered to "knit a little something we can put over his penis," Walter was horrified. *Man* was moved indoors.

Nichols described problems that soon began bubbling to the surface of the relationship, including Walter's habit of going silent when angry. She said she stopped inviting people to their home for fear that her husband, if in a bad mood, would refuse to speak to their guests. Another cause of friction was his tendency to pay bills late or, on occasion, not at all. She noted a "terrible fight" they had on the subject and believes that was the beginning of the end of the marriage. "[Walter] wasn't mean. He just didn't put himself in someone else's position."

In addition, he had very few friends. He and Peggy socialized primarily with his family or her friends, Nichols said. He never engaged in group activities such as golf, where he might have formed friendships. Ultimately, she said, she had to face the fact that art was her husband's major love in life.

At the end of October 1939, less than eighteen months after their wedding, Peggy Chrysler went to Reno. She took up residence for two months, a requirement for acquiring a divorce, on the then-standard grounds of "extreme cruelty." The divorce was granted on December 4.[27] Reno was already well-known as the place to go for quickie divorces. In Peggy's case, it took a bit longer, since she wanted to change her last name back to Sykes. She was sure this infuriated Walter, who couldn't understand why anyone would want to give up the Chrysler name.

"After the divorce, Walter's lawyers wanted to know how much money I wanted," Peggy Nichols recalls. "As it happened, one of his lawyers was an old friend of mine. He told

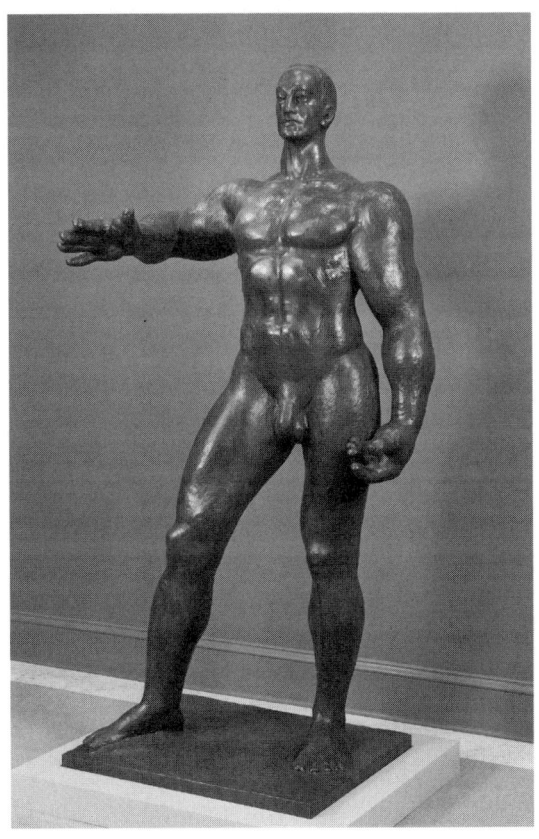

Man, by Gaston Lachaise, modeled 1930–34, cast 1938 (bronze, 100$^{1}/_{16}$ in.). The figure's anatomy caused a stir when Chrysler displayed the statue at his summer home in Long Island in the 1930s and again later, when it was posted outside the museum in Norfolk. It is currently on display inside the museum. (Chrysler Museum of Art, Norfolk, Va., gift of Walter P. Chrysler Jr. Photo courtesy of the Chrysler Museum of Art, © Gaston Lachaise/ Salander–O'Reilly Galleries, New York.)

me later that everybody was scared to death of how much I was going to ask for. I think I asked for seven thousand dollars a year for the rest of my life. And the lawyer said that after I left, they all sat down, had a drink, and breathed a sigh of relief. I didn't marry him for his money."

The Chryslers' marriage surely must have suffered for another reason entirely: Walter Chrysler was homosexual. As Vincent Curcio wrote in *Chrysler: The Life and Times of an Automotive Genius,* his 2000 biography of Walter Chrysler Sr., "in 1938, there was enormous social pressure on gay men to marry and give the appearance of living a 'normal' life. In any case, this marriage certainly was an unhappy one for both of these young people."[28]

That Chrysler led something of a double life was widely acknowledged. The fact that he was gay was noted by many of those who knew him professionally and personally. And while his sexual orientation seemed to have little bearing on his career as an art collector, it may have indirectly influenced his eventual move to Norfolk.

By the time of his son's divorce, Walter Chrysler Sr. was deteriorating at an alarming rate. He had never fully recovered from his stroke, and his wife's death shattered him. On August 15, 1940, he experienced another cerebral hemorrhage. Three days later, with his four children at his bedside, the sixty-five-year-old patriarch was dead. He was eulogized in the world press and lamented by family and friends as a great industrial leader, an automotive genius, and "an individual of enterprise and courage."[29]

Walter Chrysler Jr., Jack Chrysler, and two attorneys executed Chrysler Sr.'s will, which provided each of his four children with a quarter of his $8.8-million estate as well as real property, stocks, bonds, and individual trust funds. A year later, Chrysler Jr. purchased the North Wales Club in Fauquier

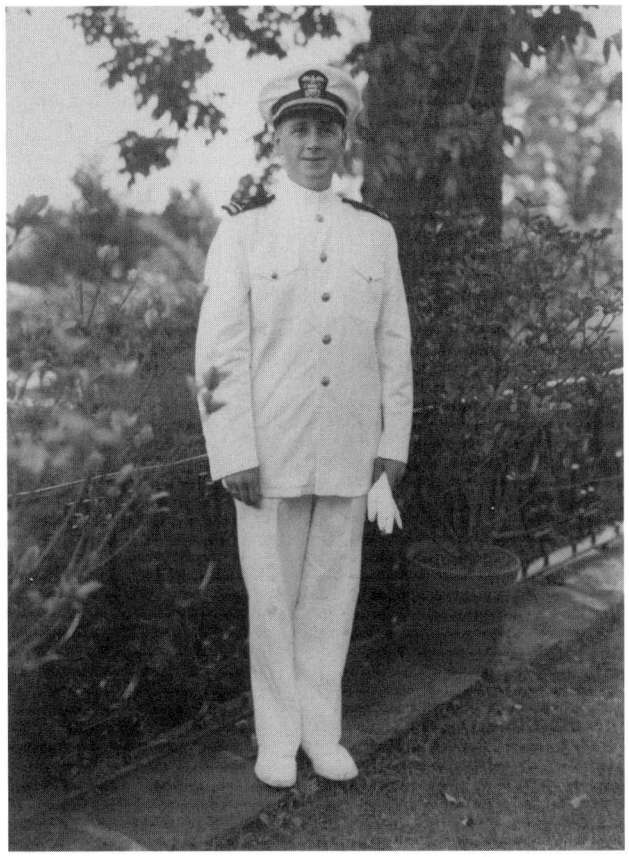

Walter Chrysler Jr. in his navy summer whites, ca. 1940s. (Courtesy of the Chrysler Museum of Art, Norfolk, Va.; photograph by Hessler.)

County near Warrenton, Virginia. The seventy-two-room mansion on 1,002 acres of land had served as a clubhouse for a group from Warrenton. The original stone house on the land had been built in 1778, and two wings had been added in 1912. North Wales, and the art it contained, cost Chrysler $176,500, but he invested some $7.5 million more into it over the seventeen years of his ownership. In a *New York Times* story about the purchase, Chrysler was identified only as a newcomer to thoroughbred horse racing who had been recently acquiring brood mares. At the time of the purchase, he owned about fifty of them.

But he had already amassed a superb art collection, and that year he showed it to the public in its entirety for the first time. The exhibit traveled to two locations: the Philadelphia Museum and, its first stop, the Virginia Museum of Fine Arts in Richmond. The show contained works by Picasso, Matisse, El Greco, Goya, Degas, Manet, Renoir, Toulouse-Lautrec, Chardin, Cézanne, Lachaise, Brancusi, Chirico, Gris, and Miró, among others. The *New York Times* called the collection "one of the largest of modern art in the United States."[30] The *Richmond News Leader,* on the other hand, had some more specific comments: "A few things to admire, a lot to hate, much to laugh out loud over, but nothing to yawn at make up the Chrysler Exhibit of Modern Art."[31]

On April 10, 1942, four months after the Japanese attacked Pearl Harbor, Walter P. Chrysler Jr. enlisted in the U.S. Navy. The thirty-two-year-old lieutenant junior grade was stationed in Norfolk. It was while based in that navy town on the southeastern coast of Virginia that Chrysler would meet a young woman who would dramatically change his, and the city's, future.

4

WALTER AND JEAN

Jean Esther Outland was born in the town of South Norfolk on September 15, 1921.[1] She was the second of Lida Maddox and Grover Cleveland Outland's four children. Jean's older sister, Louise Outland Smith, recalled how the large family struggled on their father's salary as a school principal.[2] Grover Outland eventually went into the insurance business and, for a few years after World War II, served as a member of the Virginia House of Delegates. By then, the family had moved from South Norfolk to the wealthier, more established Edgewater section of Norfolk.

Jean's younger sister, Nancy Chandler, traced what was to become Jean's lifelong appreciation of books back to their childhood. Jean used to play librarian, glue paper pockets into the family's volumes, and charge her siblings two-cent-a-day overdue fines.[3]

Jean Outland attended Maury High School and was a 1942 graduate of the College of William and Mary. For several years afterward, she taught physical education at the college's Norfolk Division, now Old Dominion University. Jean was cheerful and lively—someone, said her younger sister, who could light up a room. She was always ready for a party—and especially an opportunity to dance. Indeed, by most accounts, it was at a 1944 dance that twenty-three-year-old Jean Outland met her future husband, Walter P. Chrysler Jr. Chrysler must have looked fit in his officer's uniform that evening, his round, boyish face belying his thirty-five years.

The dance was held at the Cavalier Hotel in Virginia Beach. "It was the last time the place was open before the Navy took it over," Chrysler would later recall. "One of the ensigns in the squadron brought Jean. Looking around the table, I thought she was the only really attractive person there. So I asked her to dance," said Chrysler, "and the dirty work started."[4]

In another version, Chrysler was introduced to Outland by a young man she was dating at the time. "When her beau left for overseas, he asked Chrysler to 'take good care of Jean.' And he did."[5] Louise Outland Smith recalled her younger sister's first encounter with Chrysler as slightly less romantic: "Jean found him on a streetcar," she said. As a result of the overcrowding in Norfolk during the war, a movement began in which servicemen were invited to churches for Sunday supper. Following suit, the Outland family would set an extra place at their dinner table, and Jean was told that if she noticed a lonesome-looking uniformed soldier or sailor on a streetcar, she should invite him home for a meal. "So," said Smith, "she found Walter and brought him home one day." When he introduced himself to her father at the door, Smith added, nobody believed he was really Walter Chrysler, "but we didn't say anything." Smith said that Chrysler, twelve years her little sister's senior, seemed like an interesting person, "but I think somewhat shy, like Jean, and a little nervous."

The family dined on a Smithfield ham from their own farm, a rare treat during a period of rationing. "Walter loved that ham," Smith said. "Then the invitations started coming in." She added, "Walter was transferred to Key West, and the

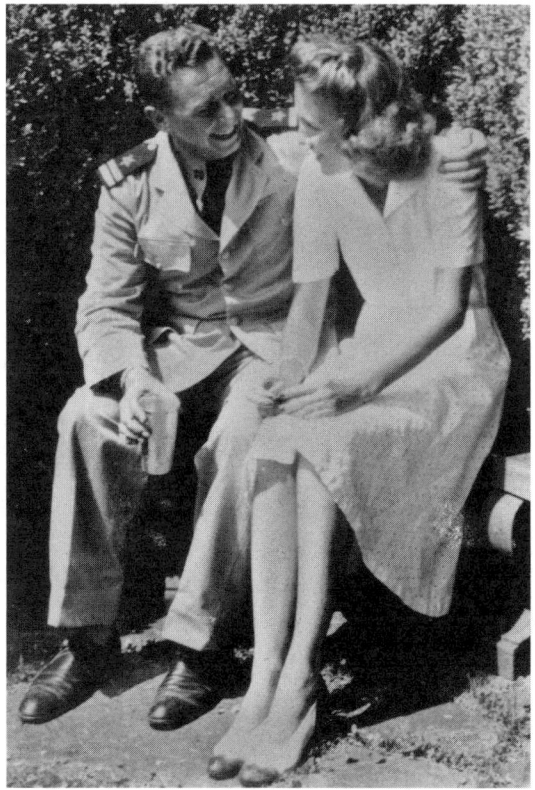

Walter, in his navy uniform, and Jean Outland, Norfolk, ca. 1940s.
(Courtesy of the Chrysler Museum of Art, Norfolk, Va.)

rumors were flying. He got out of the navy. Now, we should
have known that that was a strange thing, to be released from
the navy during wartime."[6]

Those rumors were spelled out in a 1955 *Confidential Maga-*
zine article entitled "The Strange Case of Walter Chrysler Jr."
It claimed Chrysler was forced to resign by the secretary of
the navy because he'd been having "notorious wild parties"
in his private Key West home.[7] R. L. Blazevig, a retired naval
aviator who was also based at N.A.S. Key West during World

War II, remembered instead that Chrysler was discharged because he was "found to be gay."[8] Chrysler's own explanation for his December 5, 1944, departure was a recurrence of his ulcer problems.[9]

Soon after Chrysler resigned his commission, Jean was invited to North Wales for the weekend. It was there that Chrysler proposed marriage to her. The wedding took place on a Saturday morning, January 13, 1945, in a simple ceremony at Norfolk's Freemason Street Baptist Church. The bride had no attendants and wore an aquamarine wool crepe dress.[10]

"Nobody knew it was going to happen," Smith said. "It was a big secret. That was Walter's wish." Smith recalled that the Chryslers honeymooned at the Homestead Resort in Hot Springs, Virginia, but wondered, "Why go anywhere when you've got North Wales? They had an absolutely wonderful staff; they built a swimming pool and a tennis court. It was a dazzling place," Smith said. Jean Chrysler's siblings were invited to the estate on several occasions and were amazed by the art on view. They played bridge under a Velázquez; there was a Gilbert Stuart painting of George Washington over the mantel and a Degas in the dining room. In the North Wales drawing room hung the Picasso of two women at a bar that Chrysler had bought as part of his and Gertrude Stein's scheme to help the young Parisian gallery owners.

Grover Outland recalled riding horses at North Wales while he was attending Virginia Military Institute. "I guess I was awed by Walter," Outland said, "but he was a down-to-earth type guy, and he had some great stories."[11]

There were invitations to the Chryslers' Park Avenue apartment, as well. "There's a story that Jean, when she met her first butler, asked him to tell her what to do because she'd never seen a butler before," recalled Louise Smith. Grover Outland has fond memories of visits to the Chryslers' apartments, as well. "One looked like a large home in Norfolk, but it was two or three stories on Park Avenue," he said. "I'd go up there with another guy, and we'd be out on the town and come in at night, and the butler would leave the grog tray right where you'd come in. Outside their room was the beautiful Rodin *Hands of God*. I used to hang my hat on it!"

Jean's brother and sisters were occasional guests of the Chryslers at the Metropolitan Opera, where the couple had box seats. Jean evolved into something of a connoisseur and years later would serve as a longtime trustee and executive committee secretary of the Virginia Opera Association, as well as a tireless volunteer for that organization.

Like her sister-in-law Thelma Chrysler Foy and the first Mrs. Chrysler Jr., Jean developed an affection for miniature purebred dogs. At North Wales she raised long-haired Chihuahuas, and she owned a succession of them for the rest of her life. Jean was an avid supporter of the SPCA and volunteered for them for many years.[12]

Despite the grandeur of North Wales, Jean had mixed feelings about it. In a 1956 interview, she said of the northern Virginia estate: "It is really a beautiful place, but we can stay there so little. I tried it one year. I found myself alone there with the servants except when we had guests. My husband was in New York most of the time."[13]

In addition to building his art collection, seeing to his horse farm, and sailing the yacht he bought from bandleader Tommy Dorsey, Chrysler was interested in the theater and tried his hand at producing plays. In fact, *Theatre Arts* magazine dubbed him "Broadway's newest angel" in 1952. "At a time when theatre is at its weakest financially and many investors are retreating from it as a poor risk," the magazine noted, "Mr. Chrysler has become a large-scale theatrical backer. The theatre is no mere avocation with him."[14]

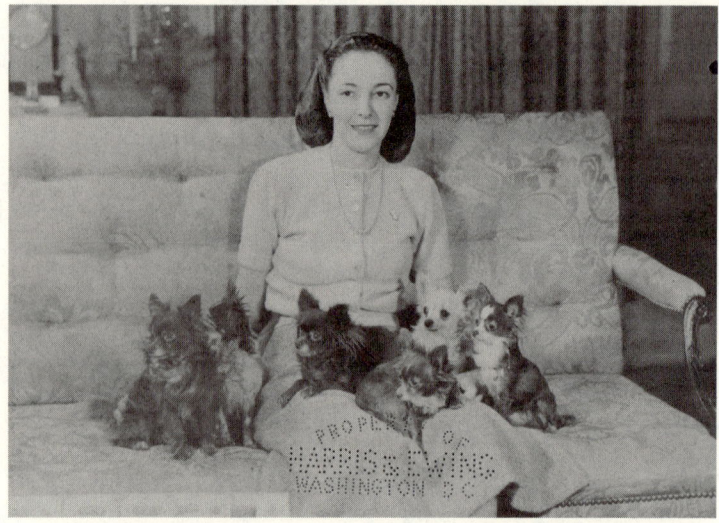

Jean Outland Chrysler, ca. 1940s, seated with her prize long-haired Chihuahuas in the living room of the majestic North Wales estate in Warrenton, Virginia, where Walter raised racehorses. This lavish lifestyle was abandoned when Walter began to work toward founding a museum. (Courtesy of the Chrysler Museum of Art, Norfolk, Va.; photograph by Harris and Ewing, Washington, D.C.)

Chrysler produced *New Faces of 1952*, a revue that launched the careers of Eartha Kitt, Paul Lynde, Alice Ghostly, and Carol Lawrence. With his coproducer, Leonard Sillman, Chrysler had "plans for a new edition of the Ziegfeld Follies." He invested in *The Hanging Judge*, a play written by the actor Raymond Massey, which was produced in London and directed by Michael Powell, who was better known for directing lyrical films like *The Red Shoes*. "I believe in the theatre," Chrysler told the magazine, "both as a playgoer to whom a good play is always a rich experience and as a business man convinced that, with proper management, fine entertainment can be made to pay its way."[15]

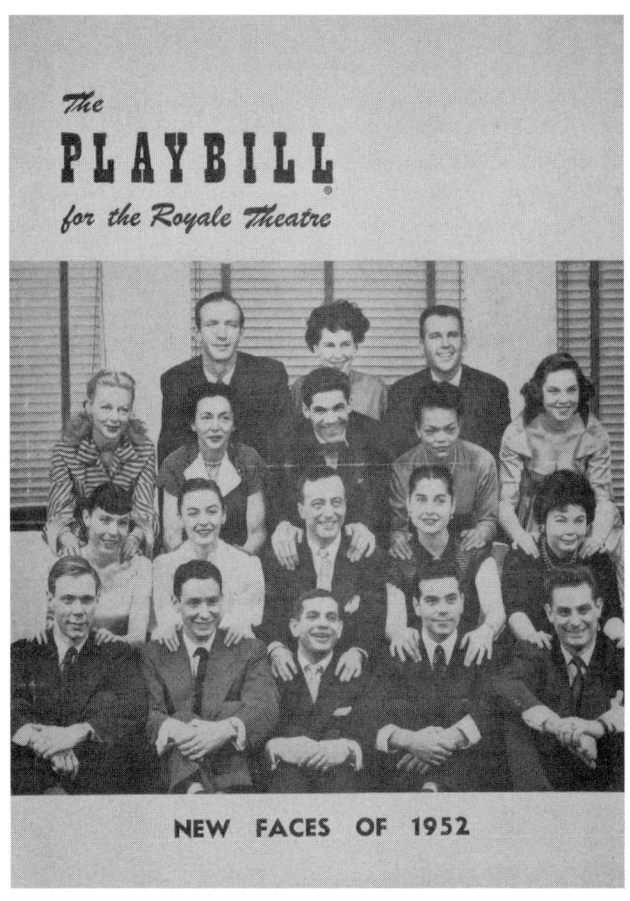

The *Playbill*® cover for the Royale Theatre, *New Faces of 1952,* a Broadway revue that Walter Chrysler produced and that introduced young performers like Eartha Kitt, Paul Lynde, and Carol Lawrence. (Photo courtesy of the Chrysler Museum of Art, Norfolk Va.; © *Playbill*®. Used by permission. All rights reserved.)

Few of the plays Chrysler backed, however, were particularly successful. In 1953, he coproduced the premiere of Tennessee Williams's *Camino Real* on Broadway. The play had a limited run, perhaps due to its inaccessible surrealism, not to mention the bashing it received from critics. In addition to his stage ventures, Chrysler produced a movie, *The Joe Louis Story.* He also served as a director of the Madison Square Garden Corporation, a position he inherited from his father.[16]

During these years, Chrysler was clearly searching for direction in his life. As his longtime friend Frank Vanderlip observed, "His ambition was to be at the top of something, but he didn't know what he could be at the top of."[17]

Chrysler bought North Wales primarily as a tax shelter, and, as such, he changed its designation over the years from racing farm to thoroughbred breeding farm to poultry farm. When, in 1957, the IRS altered its rules on tax shelters, Chrysler put the estate up for sale. It didn't sell until 1961, when a buyer purchased it for $700,000.[18]

On November 7, 1958, a family tragedy proved to be the motivation for Walter Chrysler to change the course of his life. Jack Forker Chrysler, the handsome, popular, fun-loving younger brother whom Walter adored, died of a heart attack at age forty-seven. Jack, like his father, loved beautiful women. He had married a model, but, even though the marriage produced two children, it was unhappy and caused Jack a great deal of stress. He filled his life with work and social activities; held several management positions in the Chrysler automobile business, as well as in other corporations; and was a member of the New York and American Stock Exchanges.[19]

"When Jack died," Jean would later say, "that was the turning point. Walter just suddenly looked up and said, here was

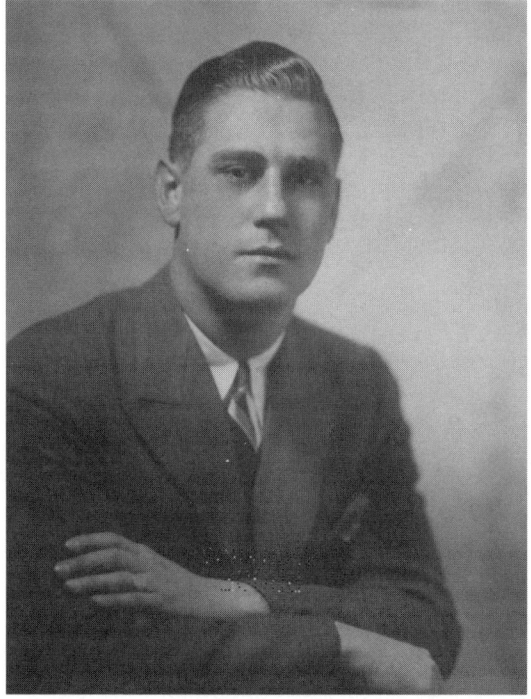

Jack Forker Chrysler, ca. 1940s. Jack was Walter's adored younger brother, whose death in 1958 at age forty-seven precipitated Walter's decision to devote his life to serious art collecting. (Courtesy of the Chrysler Museum of Art, Norfolk, Va.; photograph by Pach Brothers Studio, New York.)

this nice guy who went to all the parties and was pretty good at business, and he was in a box and had done nothing, had contributed nothing to society. I think Walter took one careful look and decided his life had to have meaning. Jack's was almost a wasted life."[20]

Jefferson C. Harrison, the Chrysler Museum's chief curator since 1993, elaborated: "Jack was more of an organization man than Walter and had none of the scandal that Walter had attached to him, because Walter was trying to live a straight life and wasn't straight. He was having a hard time with that. Even in the forties, when everything was locked down, it was still occasionally blowing up in his face."[21]

After Jack died, Chrysler "snapped into focus," said Harrison. Perhaps he felt that, as the only surviving Chrysler son, he had to make his mark. Chrysler stopped being a "gentleman collector," Harrison believes, once Jack's death made Chrysler grow up and begin working on a monument to the family.

To house that monument, Chrysler decided to move his art collection to New England, an area he knew well from his prep school and college days. The same year of his brother's death, Chrysler selected a small, picturesque town with a rich history as a summer art colony: Provincetown.

5

PROVINCETOWN

Provincetown, Massachusetts, on the northern tip of Cape Cod, had been known as an artists' and writers' enclave for decades by 1958, the year Walter Chrysler Jr. bought real estate there. According to *Ptown,* an anecdotal history by Peter Manso, from the mid-1950s onward Provincetown was well known to have an established gay community.[1]

But what particularly attracted painters was the area's dramatic setting. Provincetown forms the barb on the fishhook of the Cape, which curls seventy miles into the Atlantic, and it possesses a particularly beautiful quality of light. It is one of the few places on the East Coast where the sun sets over water. What started as a fishing village and busy seaport began welcoming marine, naturalist, and Impressionist painters in the 1890s. Abstract Expressionists such as Hans Hofmann and Franz Kline were still active when the Chryslers arrived.

To house his expanding art collection, Chrysler selected a hundred-year-old, white-shingled, deconsecrated Methodist church. The neoclassical building on Commercial Street, Provincetown's main thoroughfare, towers over its neighbors.

Chrysler paid $40,000 for the church and transformed the empty structure by removing the stained glass windows and adding showcases. Originally at street level, the building was raised onto a landscaped hill, adding to its prominence. Its conversion into the Chrysler Art Museum—nicknamed by locals "The First Church of Chrysler" or "St. Walter's"—was financed by the sale of twenty-nine Impressionist paintings in London, from which Chrysler realized $613,256. To introduce the museum and kick off its first show, he threw a black-tie party at which caterers from Boston fed Provincetown's civic leaders. There they mingled with New York art critics and Chrysler's celebrity acquaintances.

Thus began Walter Chrysler's tangible legacy, a gallery that a Provincetown newspaper reporter dubbed a "mini-Metropolitan Museum of Art."[2] The trade-off was having to abandon his previous life with all its trappings of luxury. The days of horses, yachts, and extravagant spending on clothing, jewelry, and entertaining were over. Jean did her own cooking in Provincetown and even hauled wood for the fireplaces in their home. She drove a Plymouth Barracuda on the Cape and, when in New York, rode subways or buses.[3]

Once he settled into his new lifestyle, Walter Chrysler could often be found eating breakfast at a local fishermen's restaurant. Later he might be perched on a plastic chair at his museum's open front door, wearing a sports shirt and casual slacks. He greeted visitors, took their seventy-five-cent admission fee, and occasionally escorted them on personal tours of his collection.

Depending on the theme of a summer show, Chrysler might spice up the museum's permanent exhibit with masterworks he kept warehoused in Manhattan. Provincetowners and tourists could view such dazzling gems as Matisse's *Dance*, Rouault's *Head of Christ*, or Renoir's *Daughters of Durand Ruel*, which, three decades later, would become

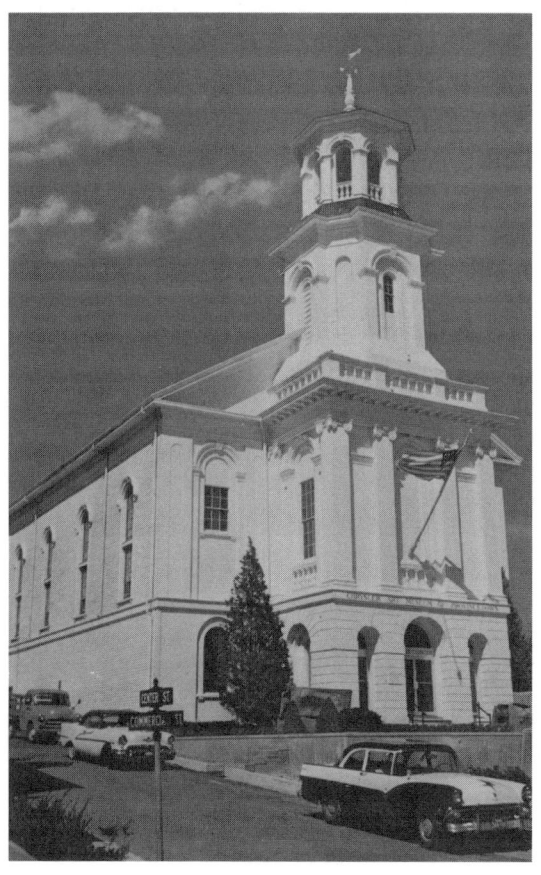

The Chrysler Art Museum of Provincetown. Walter Chrysler purchased a deconsecrated Methodist church in 1959 and converted it into the museum he maintained for twelve years, until his move to Norfolk. (Courtesy of the Chrysler Museum of Art, Norfolk, Va.; photograph by Quinn Studio.)

one of the most well-known paintings in Norfolk's Chrysler Museum.

In Provincetown, Chrysler also began compiling a large glass collection. Minna Rosenblatt was a Manhattan glass dealer who sold to him from the Provincetown days almost until his death. "When Walter wanted something, he usually got it," Rosenblatt said. She remarked on Chrysler's instincts, courage, and good taste in glass, as well as his tenacity when he selected an object, even if it was not for sale. "He said, 'I either get that or I don't take anything.' It was a form of bribery—and he got it!"[4]

Rosenblatt noted that Chrysler's enthusiasm could also lead him astray. "He did buy some things that were not right, and you couldn't be with him all the time," she said. "He was on his own. He did what he wanted when he wanted to." Rosenblatt was the source, she said, of much of the American glass now in the Chrysler Museum. Her dealings with Chrysler were always on a cash basis. She had begun making buying trips to Europe in 1957, and on one trip she purchased a delicate object in *pâte de verre,* a type of glass made from a paste fired in a mold. Rosenblatt offered the rare, tiny piece to the Corning Museum of Glass, but when they hesitated she called Chrysler. "He came down, and he bought it in a second. It's still in the museum," Rosenblatt said. She believes that when it came to glass, "Walter had the finest museum in the country."

In Provincetown, Chrysler collected paintings from local artists. He would typically visit a painter's studio and buy several pictures, sometimes the entire contents of a studio, in line with a "cheaper by the dozen" rationale. One painter whose work he acquired this way was Peter Busa, who died in 1985.

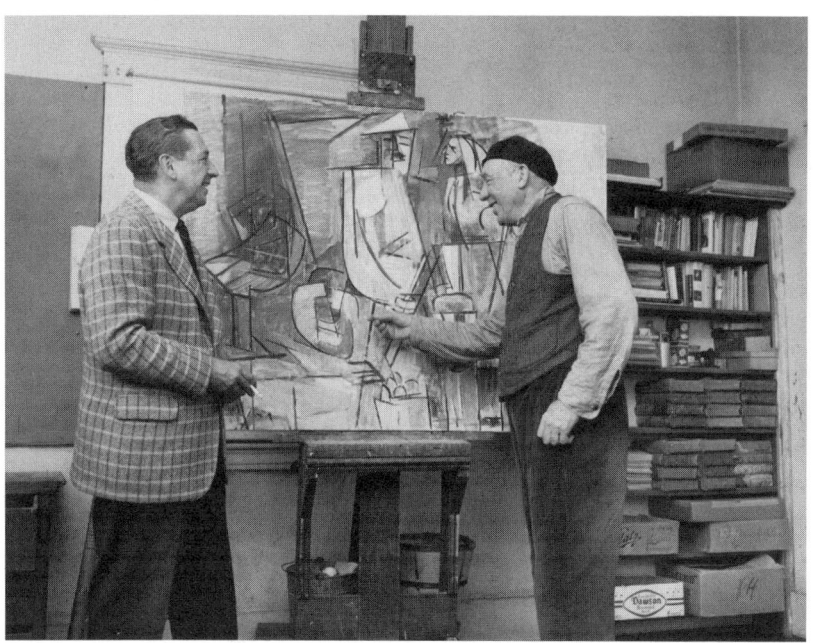

Walter and the American abstract painter Karl Knaths, in his studio in Provincetown, Massachusetts, ca. 1960s. (Courtesy of the Chrysler Museum of Art, Norfolk, Va.; photograph © Worcester Telegram and Gazette Corp.)

"Walter bought over three hundred paintings from my father, in the fifties, when my father was living [in Provincetown]," Busa's son Christopher said. Peter Busa left teaching jobs in New York City to move to Provincetown and raise his family; Christopher is the oldest of five children. During that period, he said, his father was virtually supported by Walter Chrysler's patronage. "Chrysler would buy almost an entire year's body of work. He'd buy the paintings at discount, but the artist would have an opportunity to have some regular income. My father was grateful for that."[5]

When Christopher was an adolescent, he saw Chrysler

in his father's studio; he described the older man as being short, dapper, powerful, and "like a fireplug" with a commanding presence. Chrysler's role, said Busa, was to buy an artist's paintings and sometimes donate them to small museums around the country. "It protects them," Busa said. "It was a way to scatter your seeds, and my father was always conscious of getting his things into high-level collections, as most artists are."

Busa also remembered seeing Chrysler sitting at his museum's door and collecting admission. "That was one of the jokes," he said. "He was sort of penny-wise and pound-foolish. It was silly in a way. You can't make any money selling tickets. In terms of his oddball-ness, I guess the wealth itself can make you eccentric."

One of the people who knew Chrysler best during that period was Ronald A. Kuchta, who was curator of the Chrysler Museum in Provincetown from 1962 to 1968. While he was in college, Kuchta worked on Cape Cod for part of the summer. For the rest of the season, he studied painting in Provincetown at the Cape Cod School of Art, run by the German American painter and teacher Henry Hensche. One summer on the Cape, while Kuchta was a graduate student in art history, Hensche told him about Chrysler's new museum and introduced him to its founder.

"I was just going to finish grad school the next year," Kuchta recalled. "Chrysler said, 'You could come up and work for me next summer.' So I thought that was a great compliment." The following year, Kuchta still hadn't heard from Chrysler and was about to start work on a doctorate at the Cleveland Museum and Case Western Reserve University. "I remember I was in the backyard of my parent's house in Cleveland," Kuchta said, "and my mother came out the door and said, 'Walter Chrysler's on the phone.' He said he was sorry he hadn't contacted me. He'd had bleeding ulcers and had been in the hospital for a month or two. But he needed my help immediately. How soon could I come up? I said, 'Well, the first of June?' He said, 'No! I need you next week!'"[6]

Kuchta's university advisers encouraged him to take the job, seeing it as an excellent learning opportunity. "The first day I got there, Walter had arranged a place for me to live, a nice little house owned by Karl Knaths, the painter."

Kuchta described Chrysler's impressive renovation of the church's exterior, its grand staircase and large inner spaces. "The museum was strewn with paintings," he said. "They were all on the floor and against the wall. And he said, 'Your first job, Ron, is to put these paintings in chronological order—everything from Gauguin to Picasso and Matisse and so forth.'" Kuchta said Chrysler was impressed with his work. For the young grad student, becoming a part of Walter Chrysler's world was exciting. "I was immediately thrust into the art world. It was a very heady experience, meeting all these artists and collectors: Hans Hofmann, Mark Rothko, Robert Tworkov, Robert Motherwell, Helen Frankenthaler. It was a fantastic summer."

For tax reasons, Chrysler couldn't live in Massachusetts for more than six months at a time, so when the summer ended he asked Kuchta to remain and keep the museum open. "We had a maintenance man and guards, but I was it," Kuchta said. Once again, with the blessings of his professors, Kuchta stayed on. He was involved with Chrysler's amassing of art glass. At first Chrysler only collected American, such as Cape Cod Sandwich glass, but then he began buying international glass. Kuchta remembered Chrysler returning to Provincetown, his big Dodge station wagon filled with boxes of glass objects after a day of visiting dealers.

In 1965, at Chrysler's suggestion, Kuchta hired Nancy Merrill as curator for the new "Institute of Glass," housed in an old Provincetown bank building Chrysler had purchased. Merrill's father was president of a local bank, and she had been running the family's summer hotel, the Gifford House, in Provincetown. Chrysler had known the Merrills for several years and had been a regular customer at the Gifford House restaurant.

Merrill hadn't been formally trained in art; she had studied history in college. Nevertheless, she was willing to learn about glass on the job, which she did so well that Chrysler brought her with him when he moved his collection to Norfolk.[7] Kuchta noted that Chrysler's faith in Merrill's ability provided her with a career.

This delegation of responsibility was, for Chrysler, rather uncharacteristic, considering his usual insistence on involvement in even the tiniest detail. His favorite occupation, said Kuchta, was standing and rearranging the postcard racks in the lobby. "He was determined to keep them in alphabetical order, from Albers to Zurbaran, and he was furious when people would move them around." Kuchta was often mistaken for Chrysler because his boss, who usually dressed casually, insisted Kuchta always wear a coat and tie.

One of Kuchta's fondest memories was of the time Andy Warhol and the Velvet Underground performed their "Exploding Plastic Inevitable" at Chrysler's Provincetown museum. Kuchta said that the show, which was staged every night for two weeks, attracted large crowds. "I remember Walter having a little cocktail party in his house for Andy, and he invited Hans Hofmann. I introduced Hofmann to Andy Warhol, and Hofmann, with his German accent, said, 'Vat you do is not aesthetic. I don't think you do aesthetic art.' And of course Andy, in his inimitable way, said, 'Oh really?'"

While Chrysler was at his post at the museum's entrance, his wife was out of sight, quietly laboring over her own special legacy. Jean's childhood love of books had persisted. In the museum's damp basement, she diligently organized and catalogued thousands of art volumes, folders, and clip files, which were made available to local and visiting students and scholars. Some former visitors to the Provincetown museum still smile when they describe finding Jean, in gloves, galoshes, a fur coat and hat, propped on a stool and tending to her art books in the dank, chilly bowels of the church.

"Jean was always up for a party and very jovial and sociable," Kuchta said. "She would come to the museum every afternoon and work in the library. She'd go underground. She was a great defender of Walter, very loyal. I don't know how she put up with him. She'd want a new refrigerator for their house in Provincetown, and he wouldn't buy it. He'd buy another Tiffany lamp or another Majorelle bookcase."

Kuchta recalled accompanying Chrysler to buy Tiffany lamps and Art Nouveau decorative objects—before they had become popular—from importers on Nineteenth and Twentieth Streets on Manhattan's East Side. In dealers' showrooms, Kuchta said, Chrysler would always ask for his opinion. "That was the best part of my experience." The proprietors, Kuchta said, were like rug dealers, unveiling one picture after another. Chrysler would want to know which one Kuchta preferred and why. At the same time, Kuchta recognized Chrysler's knowledge of art. "He'd seen an awful lot. He had a unique position because he was rich. Everyone would show him whatever he wanted to see and bring him things. He had a wide frame of reference." Kuchta said that Chrysler didn't do a lot of reading on art history, but he expected Kuchta to do so. "He told me that every night I should go to bed with an art history book in my hands and, if possible, have a work of art within view of my bedroom to look at before I went to bed and when I woke up. And he said I should examine the work and absorb the range of feelings and aesthetic experience it would provide by close examination over a period of time."

Kuchta remembered Chrysler offering more practical advice, as well. "Once, when we were driving on the Cape going to some galleries and antique shops, he said, 'Ron, never use me as an example for your behavior. I have a famous name, I'm a famous person, and I can get away with a lot more than you can.'"

Kuchta admired Chrysler's "rapid intelligence" with numbers, which served him well when haggling for artworks. "In his mind, because he spent almost all his time and energy and money buying art, he felt he should get the best possible deal of anyone. One of his favorite expressions was, 'What's the very *least* you will take for this?'" Chrysler might then suggest he make a series of payments over time. "He often had the dealer or the artist baffled," Kuchta said, "but because of who he was, they'd usually concede and make the deal. In the long run, it made for a lot of unhappy dealers and artists. They resented him."

Kuchta began to share that feeling when he realized Chrysler expected him to handle even the most menial tasks in the museum, from replacing the men's room toilet paper to overseeing building maintenance, without any extra compensation. "I couldn't believe it," he said. "When I finally quit, I had been there about seven years, and he never gave me a raise. I think I made five thousand dollars.

"Whenever I'd bring up the subject of raises, he'd say, 'Ron, what do you need a raise for? You have very reasonable rent. You have a lovely house to live in, a lovely view of Cape Cod Bay. Whenever Jean and I are in Provincetown, you're always welcome to have dinner with us. The museum provides you with your social life. When you're down in New York, you have a place to stay.' He'd put me up in a hotel in Gramercy Park. He said, 'You're gaining an enormous amount of experience in the art world, and you live a very good life. You don't need more money. Money isn't everything!'"

Kuchta remembered some of the New York dealers he met with Chrysler. "The art dealers Jack Tanzer and Warren Adelson did some of the earliest dealings, the trading," said Kuchta. "Walter really gave [Tanzer] his start. He sold a lot through Tanzer to Norton Simon and a gallery on Fifty-seventh Street that belonged to his brother."

Jack Tanzer, a former sportswriter who died in 2005, began collecting art after World War II. He would frequent auctions and, as he became more knowledgeable, developed what would become a long career as a successful art dealer. He had a small gallery on Madison Avenue in the early 1960s. "I got to know Walter when I opened a little gallery in Provincetown, just for one summer, about 1963 or '64," said Tanzer. He returned to New York and formed a company, Museum Art Exchange, with Warren Adelson. Most of their early business consisted of acquiring American paintings and the occasional Old Master for Chrysler, whom Tanzer virtually credited with the company's formation. "Then we started doing business with other museums," he said.

"It was all exchange with Walter. I never used any money. He didn't either. It was exchanging extra things he had for things that would fit into the collection." In 1971, Tanzer left Museum Art Exchange for a job with Knoedler's Gallery. "Then we started some big stuff," he said.[8]

Robert Kashey, who was a Manhattan gallery owner and nineteenth-century art scholar, remembers a period when Chrysler was "hanging around Madison and Third Avenues— and then he got his own shop. I knew him in a friendly way. He and Jimmy Lepere, a dealer, would buy things together and run around together. They were like partners. James was quite a character, a bit of a drunkard. Everyone had to kind of take care of him, take him by the hand and make sure he didn't destroy himself. Walter was very good to him. Walter had a great compassion—he liked that kind of seamy side of life—but with compassion. He and Jimmy worked together for a long time."[9]

Kashey recalled an incident when he and his wife were taking a walk and spotted Chrysler in a secondhand store. "Walter would always do the thrift shops. We'd all go and look for objects. And there was Walter, holding a shirt up to him. I said, 'Walter! Aren't you supposed to be looking at art instead of trying on shirts?'"

Kashey remembered Chrysler's Madison Avenue shop as "handsome. He sold paintings and sculpture, definitely fine art," he said. "Even the decorative art was museum-worthy."

Kashey found Chrysler to be "erudite and interesting," and he recalled their occasional chats at the Madison Pub. "He was so well-versed on everything—literature and music—a clever man."

6

THE COLLECTOR

Like almost everything else in his life, the way Walter Chrysler collected art was a study in extremes. Jeff Harrison summed it up: Chrysler "collected massively and unevenly. Over the course of thirty to forty years, he collected so massively that he acquired an extraordinary number of top-flight pictures. He also collected a lot of second-rate material and a few suspect things. I never got the feeling that, academically across the board, he understood what he had done."

Harrison said that Chrysler's accumulation of "one of the last great collections of European and American painting" to be formed in the twentieth century was phenomenal, "an astonishing life's record." Especially, Harrison said, considering that Chrysler had amassed two separate collections of European paintings. He sold the first one off to buy the second.

"The man never stopped," Harrison said. "In the late 1940s, he really started to shift gears. Braque, Miró, Picasso, Matisse—and here's a little Chardin out of nowhere in 1939." After World War II, Chrysler focused on more great painters of the past: Gainsborough, Rubens, Corot, Teniers. Harrison said he has copies of export licenses from Paris in the 1950s when Chrysler bought hundreds of paintings in one year. "But these are all the great ones," said Harrison. "That was the collection that was pretty much in place by the time he got to Provincetown." Harrison said that in the area of French painting, Chrysler sought advice from Robert Manning, then the director of the Finch College Art Museum in New York. Manning's wife at that time was Bertina Suida Manning, who was the daughter of the art historian William Suida. She gave Chrysler advice on Italian paintings.

But often Chrysler trusted his own eye. "I think he was moving so fast that sometimes the day wasn't long enough to get expert advice," Harrison said. "He just bought it, great stuff against the curve, Italian Baroque pictures at a time when great European collections after World War II were breaking up and very few American private collectors were looking at really important stuff coming out of England. Walter was."

When Chrysler acquired paintings by Salvatore Rosa from the Ashburnham collection in the early 1950s, the British art establishment protested. He bought Art Nouveau furniture and great nineteenth-century academic French paintings, like the museum's Bouguereau, Gérome, and Doré, at a time when most American art historians and collectors dismissed them as retrograde or kitschy. But if the collection were to go on the auction block now, noted Harrison, museums all over the world would be interested.

"It was pretty much him, sometimes with advisers, sometimes not; sometimes getting it absolutely right, [and] every now and then, getting it absolutely wrong. And not stopping long enough to know the difference. Like Leviathan with his mouth open, he just sort of swallowed it all."

In a 1980 interview, Chrysler discussed how exciting it had

been, especially in his youth, to acquire art. "These acquisitions began to form a collection that did not have a particular purpose except to provide me with enjoyment," Chrysler said. "I started to realize that there were serious implications involved in what I was doing," he added, and he "began buying paintings that would strengthen the collection as a whole." Chrysler said he considered himself fortunate to have been able to make his own decisions as a collector. "I have based my decisions on my own understandings and my own response to the artist's total oeuvre," he said.[1]

Ron Kuchta believes Chrysler always had a clear vision: To collect in quantity, ahead of the market. "He'd sell off his second-rate pieces," said Kuchta, "give a certain [number] of works to the museum and keep a certain [number] for his own apartment or house."

David Steadman, who served as the director of Norfolk's Chrysler Museum from 1980 to 1989, concurred, saying he always took Walter Chrysler seriously. Steadman recognized Chrysler's "terrific gut instinct" for certain kinds of art, particularly modern twentieth century: "No one person has an encyclopedic knowledge. So in the areas where he knew something, he was very good. In glass, he knew what he was doing. In twentieth century, he knew. Old Masters, it was kind of hit or miss. Classical antiquities, he didn't know anything, quite frankly. And African? Hmmm."[2]

The Chrysler Museum's former glass curator, Gary Baker, thought the Museum of Modern Art's Tiffany revival must have aroused Chrysler's interest in it. MoMA had a Tiffany exhibit in 1958. The following year, Chrysler bought fourteen pieces of Tiffany, which drove up the prices of the glass and sparked interest in it. Baker offered an example of Chrysler's competitiveness and compulsiveness as a collector: "Toward the end of his life he was trying to collect materials for a music library to give to the opera. He was buying scratched opera records for fifty cents and feeling very pleased.[3]

"He had substantial resources, but a point that is important to remember about him is he wasn't nearly as rich as a lot of the great collectors of the twentieth century. He did this on a comparative shoestring. With glass, he would buy anything marked, so that meant you ended up with junk glass that was mechanically blown in the 1960s that had a name on it. But he also came to Nancy [Merrill] once with a piece that was marked 'Marinot.' Well, Marinot is, in my view, one of the great people in French glass in the twentieth century; he is sometimes called the grandfather of the studio glass movement. Walter found one of these in a junk shop in New York, and he turned it up for a pittance. It's a really major object."

Chrysler was also trying to collect one of every U.S. coin of every date. He planned to leave them to his nephew. Once, when some gold pieces came up for sale at a local auction, Chrysler wanted Baker to bid on them. Baker declined. "I told him I was suspicious of them, that a couple of them might be cast Lebanese fakes, and a couple were badly worn," said Baker. "I didn't like the way they looked. But he didn't care about condition. He just wanted to get one from every year."

Chrysler's obsession with coins extended to sifting through the change in Coke and candy machines he owned, according to a former Chrysler Museum decorative arts curator, Mark Clark. Clark remarked on the way Chrysler collected silver, which he said had been one of the strengths in the collection. But Chrysler, Clark said, sold so much of it that the collection was weakened. "Then he'd turn around and buy more, kind of second-rate stuff. It wasn't museum quality. He would buy *anything*."[4]

Clark went shopping with Chrysler in New York once, but he picked out things that Chrysler thought were too expensive. Clark thought the objects Chrysler did want to buy were not up to snuff, and said so. Clark was never invited on a buying trip again. Frequently Chrysler would come back from a weekend in New York laden with shopping bags full of purchases for the museum. Former chief curator Tom Sokolowski recalled the pleasure with which Chrysler would distribute his finds on Monday mornings in Norfolk. "He would sort of announce it, and he would empty his car, and everyone would arrive, and he'd say: 'Nancy, this is for you!' 'So-and-so, this is for you!' Walter was not a great connoisseur. He had an eye, but for all his savvy, he could easily be titillated. If someone would say, 'Walter, this is the greatest blah-blah-blah,' he would take it."[5]

In a 1980 newspaper profile, Chrysler explained some of his criteria for buying a work of art. "I like the strong effort of a painter or sculptor as opposed to the soft. I like it when an artist really gets into it, when I can see the enthusiasm. These things have to reflect themselves in the collection."

"Of course," he admitted, "I like everything. I wouldn't be stout if I didn't like all kinds of food. But the most exciting thing is always the last thing." Asked if collecting art was "fun," Chrysler bristled: "The word 'fun' is not appropriate for an area of this responsibility. When you undertake to preserve for your community some of the best examples of all periods of mankind, you're attempting to educate its population. This is serious business. I have always been a serious person. I believe frivolity is admirable only in very young children."[6]

Just the same, Tony Cacalano, a one-time registrar at the Chrysler Museum, remembers that Chrysler could act frivolously, too. Periodically, Cacalano recalled seeing a rough-looking man, dressed like a derelict, come into the museum carrying a rumpled brown paper bag. "When Chrysler would see him," said Cacalano, "he'd walk over to him, and he'd look in the bag. Then he'd pull out his checkbook, write a check, and take the bag and go somewhere. I knew it was some kind of antique. He would do things like that."[7]

7

THE CONTROVERSIAL
CENTURY

In the summer of 1962, Walter Chrysler opened an exhibit he had prepared of French and American paintings from 1850 to 1950; the show was aptly titled the Controversial Century. "The *New York Times* art critic John Canaday came up and wrote a glowing review," said Ron Kuchta. In early October, when Chrysler had to return to New York, he told Kuchta to keep the museum open every day, suggesting he organize an exhibit of local artists' work that winter. All went well, Kuchta said. "Then the Controversial Century went to Ottawa."

And at Ottawa's National Gallery of Canada something happened that would indelibly stain Walter Chrysler's reputation and would follow him for the rest of his life. The newly formed Art Dealers Association of America (ADAA), alerted by a member who had seen the show while vacationing in Provincetown, came to the conclusion that 90 of the 187 exhibited works were not authentic. The ADAA went so far as to assert that some of the paintings, attributed to artists such as Van Gogh and Degas, had actually been produced in

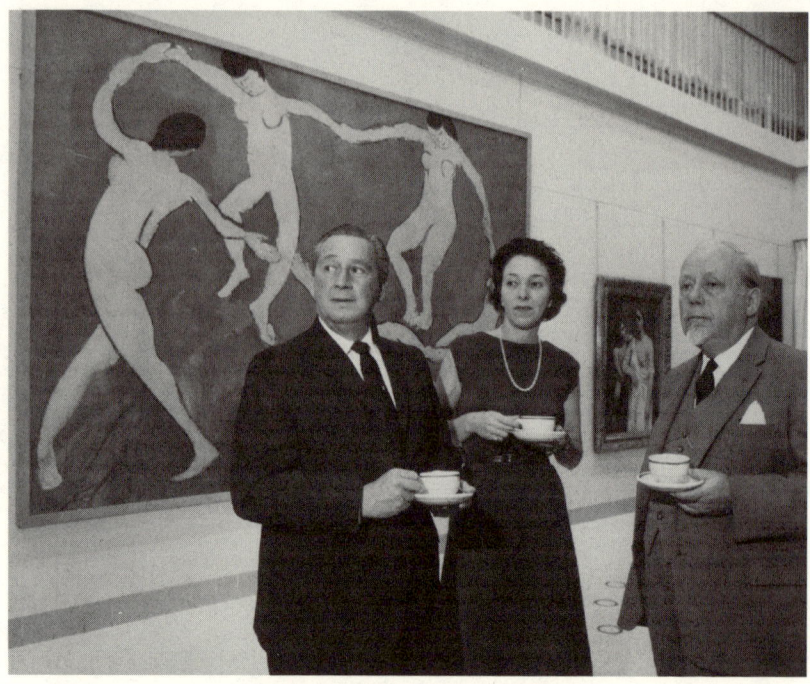

Walter, Jean, and Dr. Charles Comfort, director of the National Gallery of Canada, during the 1962 exhibition the Controversial Century, which nearly destroyed Walter's reputation. (Courtesy of the Chrysler Museum of Art, Norfolk, Va.; photograph by Dominion-Wide Photographs, Ottawa.)

the galleries from which Chrysler bought them. Worst of all, there were allegations that Chrysler was deliberately presenting these works as genuine so he could later sell them in the marketplace.[1]

The ADAA informed the Canadian museum director, Charles Comfort, of their suspicions, but Comfort insisted on proceeding with the exhibit. He explained to *Time* magazine that, thanks to all the publicity, albeit negative, crowds were pouring in to see the show in record numbers.[2]

In light of the ADAA's report, the *New York Times* had

Canaday write a new review in which he retracted his initial assessment,[3] lamely attributing his error in judgment to Cape Cod's "intoxicating air" and the ingestion of too much seafood.[4] "I got a call from the *Times* asking me to comment," Kuchta recalled. "And I said I really couldn't. I was on my own. I'd just given up my honorary scholarship at the university, and I thought, well, I'll just have to face it and see how it comes out."

Kuchta said that Chrysler's lawyer advised him not to sue for libel. "[Chrysler's] position was they were his paintings, he was satisfied with them, thinking they were by the artists he chose to think they were by," Kuchta said. "The most outstanding one, in terms of the controversy, was a painting that was supposed to be by Van Gogh. I remember that first day I arrived and arranged the collection, I questioned it myself. I'd never seen it reproduced. But, you know, Walter was a very adventurous collector, and he always liked to collect against the market and discover new things. So I gave him credit and suspended judgment. Anyway, the press really did him over at that point."

Newsweek magazine called the incident "one of the art world's most notorious affairs."[5] *Time* said it was "a scandal so big as to strike at the confidence that the art market is founded on."[6] And in a flashy *Life* magazine pictorial about the paintings in question, a bold headline shouted, "Millionaire's Fake-Riddled Picture Gallery."[7]

Chrysler blamed the ADAA. Kuchta said the organization was just being formed at that time in order to set ethical standards for the art market. Chrysler was sure he was being picked on because of his famous name but, especially, because he had enraged so many art dealers over the years. Kuchta described how Chrysler would enter an art dealer's showroom, point to a painting and declare, "'That's a Van Gogh.' It wasn't necessarily presented as such. He'd convince himself. From time to time he would bring in experts, but he was very confident in his own opinion at that stage."

Jeff Harrison viewed the Ottawa fiasco as a predictable product of "the forties and fifties, when a good many things had not been fully documented. The level of scholarship was such that you could make mistakes. You could buy what you thought was a Frans Hals but was actually a Hals school piece. That's part and parcel of the era. But there were other cases where, in the face of all evidence, he would persist. I think he thought that simply by persuasion and energy and sheer force of being a Chrysler he could make these things happen."

On its Web site, the Art Dealers Association maintains that 70 of the 187 works in the Ottawa show were misattributed.[8] Chrysler often defended the questionable pieces by saying that they were simply lesser works by the attributed artists. After all, he frequently told reporters, it would be dull if every picture painted were a masterpiece.[9]

The New York gallery owner Robert Kashey suggests Chrysler was smarter than that. "He had a flawless eye, incredible, for discovery and also for smelling when things were going to progress in the market. That takes a certain kind of talent." But in his book *False Impressions: The Hunt for Big-Time Art Fakes,* the former Metropolitan Museum director Thomas Hoving paints Chrysler with the same unflatteringly broad brush as other famous collectors, such as William Randolph Hearst, Henry Clay Frick, and J. P. Morgan: "The recipients of the new wave of fakes were the superrich, untutored industrialists and media moguls who equated art collecting with social distinction, righteousness and the American Way."[10]

Kuchta argues that the outstanding Provincetown exhibits that followed over the years more than made up for the Ottawa incident and that "the controversy kind of faded away." But did it? Nearly three decades later, the *New York Times* would dredge up the 1962 scandal in its obituary of Chrysler.[11] As with so many things in his life, questions remain: Was he an innocent victim of sly dealers? Or was he complicit in presenting the frauds as genuine?

In the case of the *New York Times,* chance played a role in wiping some of the tarnish off Chrysler's reputation. In 1991, the *Times* art critic John Russell was in Norfolk, attending an Eastern Virginia Medical School treatment program for stuttering. While there, he visited the Chrysler Museum, after which he wrote an unconditionally enthusiastic review.[12]

When he heard about Russell's article, Kuchta said, "Isn't that wonderful? Finally being vindicated. I always thought Walter would have to be dead a while before he could be appreciated."[13]

8

LEAVING PROVINCETOWN

By the late 1960s, Walter Chrysler's relationship with the people of Provincetown was deteriorating. His frequent requests for tax breaks and for a new site for the museum, a parking lot, and even a parking space for his car were denied. The town's selectmen, Chrysler charged, were not willing to support the art community sufficiently.[1]

The townspeople had just as many gripes with him. He had alienated them from the start with his cavalier attitude toward bill paying. Reminiscent of his first wife's complaints of Chrysler's disregard for others' financial needs, dealers, artists, and even the proprietor of the local hardware store were demanding money. Between 1955 and 1961 alone, Chrysler was named as a defendant in forty lawsuits for sums as small as forty dollars and as large as twenty thousand dollars.[2]

Locals thought Chrysler put himself above them. Besides, their small town simply didn't have the resources to support his museum in the ways he had expected.[3] It didn't help that Chrysler took a public stance against the creation of a national seashore on the Cape, something the majority of Provincetowners supported. The Chryslers, in turn, may not have liked the fact that Provincetown seemed to be transforming, becoming increasingly touristy and flamboyant.[4]

Even if his relations with the town had been flawless, a more practical consideration was that Chrysler's collection was becoming too large for the building on Commerce Street. It contained over one thousand paintings, many of them enormous, and many of the decorative art objects meant for display had never even been unpacked from their crates. So, in early 1970, Chrysler made it official and told the press that rising costs and the need for expansion forced him to consider closing the Chrysler Museum unless better local support was forthcoming.[5] It was not.

"At one point," Ron Kuchta said, "when he was looking around for another place before I left, we were investigating New Bedford, Massachusetts, and we were having discussions with them. When I was offered a job at the Santa Barbara Museum, [Walter and I] went to lunch, and I told him I was accepting the other job. He said, 'I understand you might want a new experience, but don't stay out there too long. There's nothing happening on the West Coast.'"

Many of the town's summer residents tried hard to "save the museum," according to *Provincetown Painters,* a book written by Dorothy Gees Seckler and edited by Kuchta. Seckler explains that the locals hated to see all the wonderful art leave town and worried that the lovely church building would end up as "some sort of neon-lit temple of tourist novelties."[6]

Alas, the sad refrain of controversy again could be heard in the background of Chrysler's life. He was accused of sneaking away from town in the night like a thief. Some saw his leaving as an act of anger; others, more generous, saw it as purely practical. None could deny, however, that the very existence of Chrysler's museum in Provincetown had inspired the opening of new galleries and increased tourism.[7] Michael Botehlo, the town manager at the time, said that the museum "brings to Provincetown the kind of tourists we want and need. Without it, there is not much in Provincetown to interest upper middle-class people."[8] Kuchta agreed, "The museum really provided a great social life for the town. It's never been the same since Walter left."

But there are some people in Provincetown who, to this day, become irate at the mere mention of Walter Chrysler. Jane Kogan's story has become almost legendary. A painter, Kogan attended a 1991 auction of eighty-nine paintings Chrysler had bought from Provincetown artists. The Chrysler Museum in Norfolk had decided to deaccession—or sell off—the pictures, which had been in storage since Chrysler's arrival.

The night of the Provincetown auction, an emotional Kogan told the crowd she was just one of many artists who had been "ripped off" by Walter Chrysler. Not only had he never paid for the two paintings he bought from her, but, except for a one-day exhibit in Provincetown, the pictures had remained hidden in storage for twenty years. Kogan asked her colleagues and neighbors to allow her to buy back one of her paintings for twenty-five dollars. When it was held up, she called out the number. Nobody bid against her. A tearful ovation followed the auctioneer's cry of "SOLD!"[9]

The nineteenth-century building that began as a Methodist church and was twice reincarnated—first as the Chrysler Museum and then as the Provincetown Heritage Museum—underwent a multimillion-dollar renovation. It now houses Provincetown's public library. But before its completion, an unsightly chain-link fence surrounded the building and its grounds. The church's cupola, like a giant doffed hat, had been temporarily removed and sat awkwardly on the lawn.

In front of the building, in a protected niche facing the street, was Chaim Gross's bronze sculpture *The Tourists*. It is a casting of the original that once stood outside Norfolk's Chrysler Museum and, in 1983, was moved to the city's Elizabeth River waterfront, where the mismatched couple still gazes across the harbor. It has been said that the bronze figures of a squat, rotund man standing beside a much taller, stately woman, were inspired by Walter and Jean Chrysler.

9

FINDING A NEW HOME

When word got out that Walter Chrysler was seeking a new home for an art collection purported to be worth $65 million, offers from museums came pouring in. In one magazine interview, Chrysler said he had received 147 applications. He explored about fifty of them, including museums in Denver, Houston, and Oakland, California.[1]

Ron Kuchta was working in Santa Barbara by then, and he invited Chrysler to visit and consider that museum. The museum was funded primarily by trustees who had been its founders in the 1930s, however, and they weren't willing to agree to Chrysler's stipulation that it carry his name. The expense of shipping his collection across the country was also cited as a reason negotiations failed.[2]

Then Norfolk's mayor, Roy Martin, heard from a former Maury High School classmate. Jean Chrysler phoned Martin and said her husband was looking for a permanent home for his collection. In an unpublished memoir, Martin wrote that Chrysler "wanted to know if we were interested in his bringing his collection to our Norfolk Museum of Arts and

Sciences. Without hesitation I said of course we were interested."

Bob Mason remembered it differently: "[Norfolk Museum director Bryan] Caldwell wrote confidentially to Mayor Martin on July 28, 1969, that Chrysler was interested in moving his museum to Norfolk." Caldwell told Martin he hadn't discussed the idea with any Norfolk Museum trustees but proposed that the city construct an eleven-story building for "The Chrysler Museum of Art."

"Caldwell vouched for the Chrysler collection's quality," wrote Mason. He had viewed it during two recent visits to Provincetown. Caldwell listed the museum's holdings under the headings of "Chinese and Japanese Art," "Near-Eastern Art," "Ancient Glass," "Statuary," "African Art," "Pre-Columbian Gold," "Glass Institute," and "Decorative Art," as well as an art reference library.

While Martin wasn't convinced that a skyscraper museum building would work, he was enthusiastic at the potential draw Chrysler's art could have for tourism. On the other hand, Mason wrote: "Judge Parker, getting wind of the Caldwell letter, saw in the same collection a threat to the community museum he loved and nurtured; further, he trusted neither Chrysler's motives nor his arithmetic. 'The trouble with Chrysler is that he's run out of museum space and wants rent-free quarters,' he snorted to a reporter. 'Sixty-five million! His junk isn't worth sixty-five dollars.'"[3]

Chrysler was still undecided when his wife called Mayor Martin, urging him to act quickly if he wanted Norfolk to have a good chance.[4] John L. "Jack" Gibson, a Norfolk banker and chairman of the Norfolk Community Promotions Commission at that time, received a phone call from Martin: "He said, if you think well of it . . . you might go up there and talk to Mr. Chrysler."

Gibson agreed to fly to Provincetown and called Denzil Skinner, who was director of the Promotions Commission, and suggested they charter a plane to look at Chrysler's collection.[5] Skinner, who would later cite Gibson's insight and intuition as critical to the campaign to get Chrysler to Norfolk, accompanied Gibson to Provincetown. "This was about 1969," Skinner recalled. "And Walter met us at the airport, and he was driving about a 1949 beat-up Plymouth sedan.[6] This car didn't even have a handle on the door of the passenger side. I was invited to ride in the front seat, and I had to get in on his side of the car and scoot across the steering wheel over a stack of newspapers in his seat." Skinner said that after Chrysler parked his car in front of the church/museum, he put a nickel in the meter. After the men strolled around the museum and admired the art for a while, Chrysler announced, "Wait a minute. I need to go back outside. I need to check the meter." When Skinner asked Chrysler why he worried about the meter, Chrysler told him that the town had refused to give him a parking space so he refused to put any more money in the meter than was absolutely necessary.

Chrysler took his visitors to the museum's musty basement, where Skinner saw what he assumed were very valuable paintings stacked up everywhere. From there they went to "an old garage-type building" crammed with more works of art, at which point Skinner asked, "Walter, do you have insurance on any of this?" and Chrysler replied: "Oh, you can't get insurance on this kind of thing."[7]

In August 1970, Norfolk mayor Roy Martin arranged for Chrysler to come to Norfolk for negotiations. Martin would later recall that Chrysler met with fifteen of "Norfolk's movers and leading members of the community" to discuss his proposal that the name Norfolk Museum of Arts and

Sciences be changed to the Chrysler Museum, to which the city would add a wing at a cost of at least $1 million. The addition would provide space for Chrysler's enormous glass and art collections.

When Chrysler arrived in Norfolk, Martin took him to meet the city manager, Thomas Maxwell. The men discussed the building of the Scope convention center with the yet-unnamed concert theater. "Without warning me," wrote Martin, "Maxwell just said, 'You know, Mr. Chrysler, I believe that Council would be very happy to name that new theater the Chrysler Hall.' . . . Needless to say, you could almost pick me up off the floor when the suggestion was made." Chrysler, delighted by the offer, leapt on it. Martin then introduced him to the other men invited to the gathering.[8]

But first Martin took Chrysler into Maxwell's office to get acquainted, said Jack Gibson. "And Roy came out while I was explaining to the bigwigs of Norfolk, saying, 'Now we gotta sell this guy!' Roy says, 'Jack! Shut up!' At which point, Maxwell came out of his office with his arm around Chrysler. "And the damn deal is done," said Gibson. "It is *done*! So when somebody asks you who was responsible for Walter Chrysler moving his collection to Norfolk? Tom Maxwell."

Martin wrote that he wanted to keep the news of the name change under wraps for a while, worried about what objections there might be by the leadership of the Norfolk Museum of Arts and Sciences to what they might perceive as "their private club" being usurped.

"Walter made a very fine presentation stating that he would be giving the City of Norfolk between $65 million and $85 million worth of art at the beginning," wrote Martin. Then Martin had his secretary call the media to say that Walter Chrysler was in Norfolk and would be making a statement before he returned to Provincetown. At an airport news conference, Chrysler announced his gift. "I believe having

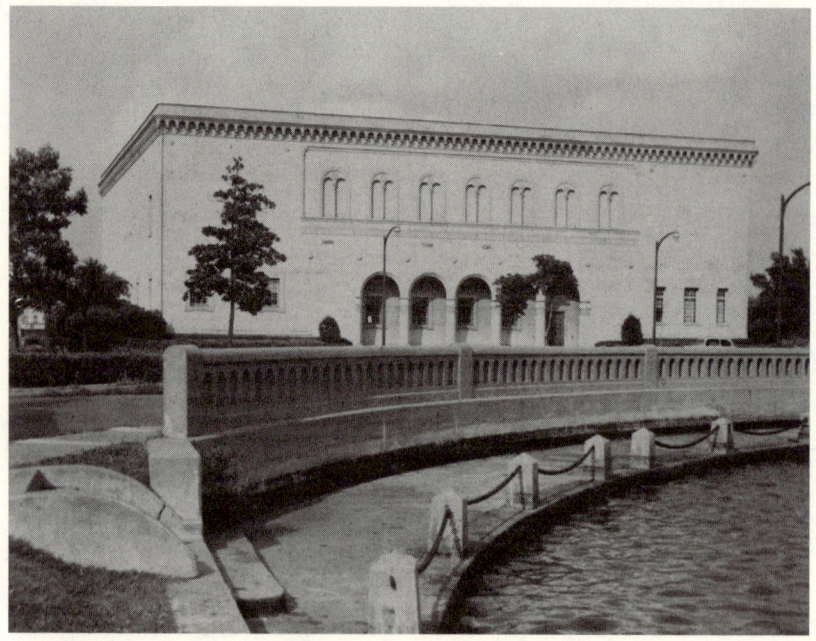

View of the Norfolk Museum of Arts and Sciences from The Hague inlet, 1951. (Courtesy of the Chrysler Museum of Art, Norfolk, Va.)

Walter on tape at the press conference kept the agreement in place," Martin later wrote, "for at times it got right shaky."

Back in Provincetown, Chrysler was interviewed about his decision. He said that in addition to moving the collection, he was considering leaving his summer home in Cape Cod and buying a house in Norfolk.[9] "I think I'm making the right move this time," he said. "The community itself is progressive. I have been assured the city as a whole is receptive to the idea of my collection moving there, and I fully expect to get the community support in Norfolk that I did not receive here."

Chrysler also saw Norfolk as having many of the amenities necessary to qualify as his collection's permanent home. It was a major port city in a region acknowledged as one of the fastest-growing in the South, and it supported two railroads.[10]

In November 1970, Mayor Martin, perhaps as way to convince skeptical board members of the Chrysler collection's value, arranged for several of them, including Judge Parker, to fly to Provincetown.[11] "Four accepted," Mason wrote, "Parker, Mrs. [Elizabeth N.] Poerstel, [Charles F.] Burroughs, and I. A four-seat airplane was chartered for us." The party arrived at the Chrysler Art Museum and found its creator sitting at a card table near the door, selling tickets, Mason recalled. "He wore, as often he did, a blue-with-white-stripes double-breasted suit that made him look like a diplomat from some little monarchy where people tended to be short, well-fed, and florid. He invited us, with an air of indifference, to look about as we wished at whatever pace suited us. Parker planted himself in front of a painting set on an easel near the entrance," while the others perused the collection. After a couple of hours, when Mason returned to the ground floor, he saw Parker still standing in the same spot where he had left him, his eyes fixed on the same painting. "Judge stood there, glowering, his thick shoulders hunched, his feet well spread," Mason wrote. Then Parker growled, "This goddamn thing is a fake!"

In Norfolk, Parker latched onto another objection. As a "charitable trust," the Norfolk Museum board wasn't legally empowered to make the dramatic changes demanded by Chrysler, he said, and he filed a legal brief to that effect.[12] By then, Bryan Caldwell had resigned as the Norfolk Museum's director and was replaced by a retired naval officer, Captain

Lee W. Mather. Less than a year later, Mather announced that he, too, was leaving. He had received high marks for the financial and administrative changes he made at the museum, but there had been friction between him and museum staffers, who criticized him "for making decisions involving artistic matters of which he has no understanding." Mather's resignation was accepted, effective January 1, 1971, and a committee was appointed to look for a qualified successor.[13]

Just ten days later, another retired navy captain, Frederick H. Wahlig, was appointed museum administrator. Wahlig, who had been an administrative assistant to City Manager Thomas Maxwell, had no prior experience in art or museums. The board felt that a "caretaker-type administration" would be practical during the transition period after Chrysler's arrival. Wahlig was hired for six months, part of that time to be served alongside Mather, who happened to be an old Naval Academy buddy of his.[14] As it happened, Wahlig stayed on until his retirement in September 1976. And, thanks to a trend toward greater professionalism, he was the last Chrysler administrator to come aboard without a museum-related background.

10

THE CITY REACTS

A month after Mayor Martin's announcement that Walter Chrysler would move his collection to Norfolk, Judge Parker had news of his own. He wrote a confidential letter to the board signaling his intention to resign in the fall, a year before his term was due to end.

By then, of eight board members, only Chrysler and Bob Mason wholeheartedly agreed with the mayor's now-public plan. Jack Roper, Charles Burroughs, and James Devereux were on the fence. Strongly opposed, like Parker, were the only two women board members, Elizabeth N. Poerstel and Virginia L. Tunstall. Tunstall's late husband had been legal adviser to the Norfolk Society of Arts and had drafted the Norfolk museum's charter.

Julie Dalton, who was vice president of the Norfolk Society of Arts at the time, was particularly surprised that Elizabeth Poerstel voted with Parker. Dalton remembered that when Poerstel first learned about Chrysler bringing his art to Norfolk, the idea of any objections to it surprised her. "Who," she asked Dalton, "would be against Santa Claus?"[1]

Now, with Parker's decision to resign, the board was eager to move on. Mason wrote that he and Burroughs agreed that Jack Roper should become president. Roper assented. The men met with Parker (the four comprised the executive committee) in October 1970 to make the change official. Parker sadly spoke about his seventeen-year tenure on the board, most of them as president, and how demanding the job had become lately. He expressed gratification that Roper, such a worthy successor, was to take his place.

"'I certainly appreciate this honor,' [Roper] said, 'but I don't know, Judge. Your legal advice and experience are going to be missed during this Chrysler business that seems to be coming up.' 'All right,' interjected Judge, brightly, 'I agree to stay!' The Hon. Roy B. Martin Jr.," Mason wrote, "had a fight on his hands."

Out to convince board members and the local press that Chrysler's collection was littered with forgeries, Parker had been circulating copies of the 1962 *Life* magazine story about the Controversial Century exhibit. Martin's response to Parker's efforts to denigrate the collection was to hire appraisers from Sotheby Parke Bernet galleries in New York. The experts assessed sixty-nine samples from Chrysler's enormous art and glass collection. They estimated the samples' worth at $5.5 million.

Parker wasn't fazed. In November, he presented the board with a forty-page document titled "Opinion" that quoted liberally from the museum's charter as well as other official documents. The paper formalized Parker's objections regarding the museum's status as a "charitable trust." According to Mason, Parker suggested that anyone who disagreed with his findings hire his own lawyer. Mason protested. The board, he said, was essentially a city agency and therefore should rely on the city attorney's office for legal counsel. No one agreed. Burroughs said he would seek advice from his company's attorney, Richard B. Spindle III, a member of Norfolk's largest law firm.

Spindle wrote a memorandum to Burroughs on February 4, 1971, in which he agreed with Parker that "the Norfolk Museum of Arts and Sciences is a *charitable trust* . . . created by joint action of the City of Norfolk and the Norfolk Society of Arts," but Spindle also insisted that "the proposed changes of name and structure of trustees in consideration of the acquisition of such a substantial gift (as Chrysler offered) could only be considered to be in furtherance of the purpose of the Museum."

The museum board's first order of business was to ratify the city council's appointment of Henry Clay Hofheimer II to fill its vacancy. Hofheimer, an industrialist who collected porcelain, had once been a trustee, but, Mason wrote, he "resigned during the Caldwell years in a disagreement with Parker. Aha!"

Roper and Burroughs offered resolutions to the board to express satisfaction with the quality of the Chrysler art and to agree to the conditions that included the city's addition of a $1-million museum wing. The first resolution was approved five to four, the second six to three. In a surprise turnaround, Devereux, after having consistently voted with Parker, Tunstall, and Poerstel, joined Chrysler, Roper, Burroughs, Mason, and Hofheimer. Mason wrote that the documents regarding the museum's transformation had to be signed by Parker, as president, and Poerstel, as secretary. Instead, Roper adjourned the meeting.

A few days later, Roper and the others who had voted in favor of the changes went over Parker's head and ordered a special board meeting to sign the papers. On April 19, in the absence of Parker, Tunstall, and Poerstal, a meeting was held. Parker sent a note to the majority insisting that his presence, as well that of the two dissenting trustees, was negligible. In fact, at such a meeting, he wrote, their roles would be reduced to "that of spectators."

With Roper presiding, the six trustees who did attend voted unanimously to approve the Chrysler contract and deed to the Provincetown art. At the next regular board meeting, the newly doubled membership would elect members and committees as set forth in the new bylaws. In August 1971, Parker filed suit in Norfolk Circuit Court against the city, the museum board's six-member majority, and even the Norfolk Society of Arts, whose membership had approved the museum changes by a majority of eleven votes.

The six board members hired Richard Spindle to represent them in the suit. He was joined by Philip Trapani, the assistant city attorney. Bob Mason recounted how a Norfolk artist painted large badges with the words "Save the Museum 6" on them, a takeoff on the slogan about the "Chicago 7" after the 1969 Democratic National Convention riots. Mason and a few others wore the badges during lunch at the private Virginia Club soon after Parker filed his lawsuit. When he saw them, wrote Mason, "Judge Parker, who was a club fixture, managed a grin." After Parker's term ran out, Tunstall and Poerstel adopted a resolution to salute and thank him, proclaiming their admiration and affection for him in perpetuity.

When Jack Roper was elected chairman of the board in May 1971, Walter Chrysler was appointed president and chief executive officer with direct supervision over the museum director. Henry Clay Hofheimer was named vice president. The nine additional board members included Chrysler's brother-in-law, Colonel Edgar W. Garbisch; Chrysler's good friend Frank A. Vanderlip Jr.; and James Brown, director of the Virginia Museum of Fine Arts in Richmond.

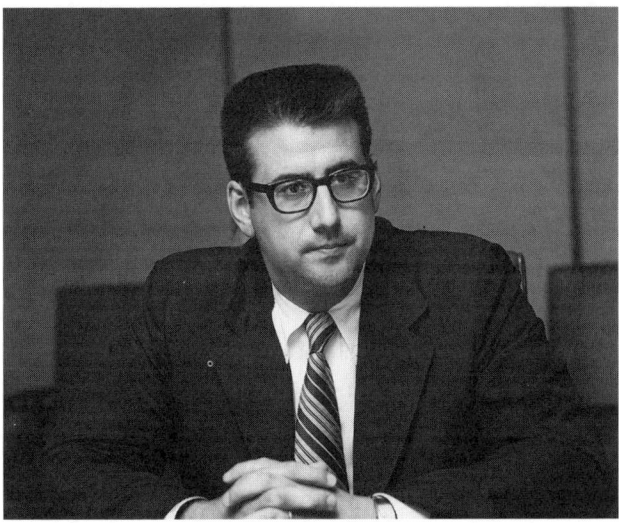

Norfolk city attorney Philip Trapani, 1974. Trapani was one of the few lawyers Walter trusted, and the only one with whom he was willing to sign the disputed codicil to his will. Trapani's emergency surgery postponed the signing, and Walter died before the rescheduled appointment, to the dismay of the museum staff and the Hampton Roads communities. (Courtesy of the *Norfolk Virginian-Pilot*.)

Among museum administrator Frederick Wahlig's first duties was to establish an insurance consortium to raise the museum's coverage from $1.5 million to $26 million and to beef up security by adding guards and sealing a door and a couple of windows.

In Mason's view, the trustees were wise to make Chrysler the interim director, as well as president, without pay. They hoped that he would do some initial reorganizing before they searched for a permanent director. They also hoped he would weary of the demanding job and be ready to leave it before long. That this might later prove an issue never occurred to them. Mason predicted (accurately, as it turned out) some of the problems a future museum director might face. He would have to be prepared for Chrysler's mercurial personality: "that he could be insightful and reasonable," but that "he also could be moody, impulsive, and explosive."

The board paid scant attention to Bryan Caldwell's mention of Chrysler's Provincetown habit of trading art to upgrade the museum's collection. Additionally, the board ignored Parker's disagreement with the "contractual right reserved by Mr. Chrysler of 'editing and exchanging'" pieces of the collection during his lifetime. This oversight would soon come back to haunt them.[2]

Parker stood before Judge Thomas M. Johnston to plead his case on December 11, 1972. Despite the argumentative tone of his brief, Parker spoke calmly in court. Richard Spindle responded in kind. Judge Johnston's decision of December 20 held that "charitable trust" did not technically apply to the situation since the Norfolk Society of Arts intended to elect a board with the authority to manage the museum. He concluded that the public's interest had "been well and properly served by the defendants' action, and dismissed the plaintiffs as 'three dissatisfied trustees.' Parker accepted the verdict with grace and announced he would not appeal."[3]

Jack Roper was chairman of the board of the Chrysler Museum at Norfolk in March 1973 when he was notified by Richard Spindle that the period for appeal by Parker had passed. Judge Johnston's ruling was final. Mrs. Tunstall and Mrs. Poerstel stayed away from board meetings for the rest of their terms.

Conflicts came and went at the new Chrysler Museum, but none ever equaled the disruptive dramatics of the Judge Parker lawsuits. Years later, Walter Chrysler referred in a speech to that combative period with the sort of humor that comes only with the passage of time. "Among my artistic peregrinations of the fifties," Chrysler said, "I produced a play in London entitled 'The Hanging Judge,' little realizing then the shadow it would cast years later in Norfolk, Virginia. But I have come to respect that phrase from the Sermon on the Mount: 'Judge not that ye be not judged.'"[4]

11

THE CHRYSLER MUSEUM AT NORFOLK

During the summer of 1971, a large portion of Walter Chrysler's art collection was transported from Provincetown and New York City to Norfolk. By that time, Norfolk had mostly recovered from its wartime honky-tonk reputation. Gone were the sailor bars and burlesque shows that had made downtown and its Elizabeth River waterfront sleazy, noisy, and dangerous.

Nevertheless, Norfolk was still very much a city in transition. Federally funded urban renewal meant that Ghent, the neighborhood in which the museum is located, was still being razed and rebuilt. Thousands of African American families—many of them moved into scattered housing projects—were displaced in the process. The Norfolk Redevelopment and Housing Authority had declared Ghent a conservation area seven years earlier, so many of the elegant early-1900s-era houses that had been divided into apartments were being restored to grand one-family homes.

Downtown Norfolk, while containing a large number of department stores, boutiques, movie theaters, and restaurants, as well as banks and office buildings, still sorely lacked adequate hotel and residential space. A 1971 editorial called Granby Street, Norfolk's "main shopping street," "shabby, poor competition for the new shopping malls where there are benches, an absence of motor vehicles, cleanliness, and tasteful design." The Elizabeth River waterfront was described as neglected and deteriorating.[1]

Culturally, Norfolk was still in its infancy. It would be several years before professional opera and theater venues would be established. The overall impact of the 1971 arrival of Walter Chrysler's art to Norfolk and Hampton Roads cannot be overemphasized. The *New York Times* called Chrysler's gift "one of the strongest and most various ever given at any one time by a single individual to an American museum."[2]

Linda Kaufman, a longtime trustee of the Chrysler Museum and one of Henry Clay Hofheimer's daughters, recalled watching the bulk of the art being delivered. "I remember when those seven big Santini Brothers trucks came down," she said of the $140,000 move.[3] "Things started to come off the trucks and be propped up against the walls, including that enormous Degas dancer. "Mr. Chrysler and I began chatting, and I probably said something brilliant like, 'Tell me about this picture.' And he said, 'You know, Linda, I paid $10,000 for that frame.' He told me how much the frame cost! I thought that was extremely unusual."

A story in *Town and Country* magazine reported, with condescension, the local reactions to the new arrivals:

> Some knew the names of certain painters— Breughel, Rubens and Rembrandt. Others were familiar with Van Dyke, Reynolds and Gainsborough. The French contingent, all of them, strangely, descendants of the Marquis de Lafayette, doted on Boucher, Delacroix and those naughty Impressionists, including Gauguin. They were even familiar with Millet, Courbet and

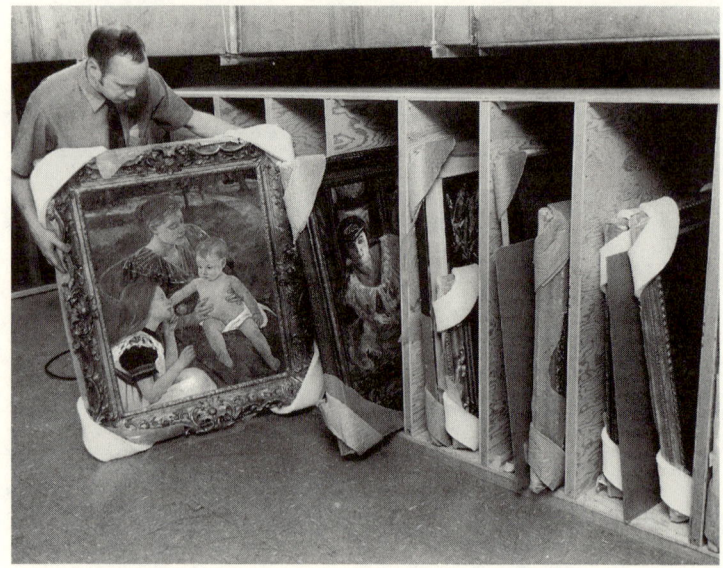

A Mary Cassatt painting, just unloaded from the initial shipment of art from Walter Chrysler, is stored by Robert B. Tonkin, chief curator at the newly named Chrysler Museum at Norfolk, in 1971. (Courtesy of the *Norfolk Virginian-Pilot*.)

Bouguereau. Italians, operating radar equipment at NATO or fruit stalls downtown, were bowled over by the Renaissance and Baroque paintings, *bello, che bello!* Finally the Daughters of the American Revolution had to fan themselves and exchange mints, such was their delight over George Caleb Bingham's "General Washington Crossing the Delaware."

"But, my dear," one Daughter was heard to mumble to another. "What is that statue outside facing the front entrance? Lachaise did you say? Well it's a fact the French are seldom responsible and rarely moral. So Lachaise is the sculptor and the model is a man called Lincoln Kirstein? But he is a gentleman, surely. A writer, a philanthropist, a man of means? To think he posed nude! Of course he's a Yankee."⁴

The effect of the marvelous new additions was put into perspective years later, as *Port Folio* magazine reported: "[Chrysler's] collection fueled the Museum, propelling it into the ranks of the major regional institutions in the country. It has been compared quite favorably with the privately accumulated treasures contained in the Barnes Foundation near Philadelphia and the Philips' Collection in Washington."⁵

Jean Chrysler's art library had grown to some fifty thousand volumes by the time it was relocated to Norfolk, though it would take eighteen years for all of it to be permanently installed within the museum. Nancy Merrill made the move from Provincetown, too, along with crates containing fifteen thousand glass objects, including priceless pieces from ancient Egypt and Rome. Most of the glass arrived by car, including one of the largest accumulations of Tiffany pieces in the country, as well as many cases of New England Sandwich glass. A great deal of the collection would not be displayed because there simply wasn't enough room.⁶

Kirkland Clarkson, an environmental activist who spent years as a docent at the museum before Chrysler's arrival, was one of several who continued in the role under the new management. "We didn't have an education director [the former director, Richard Carroll, had resigned in 1969], so we had to do our own research and write our own scripts," Clarkson said. "And then we had to find out what they were learning in the schools and what did we have at the museum that would tie in." Eventually, the Junior League paid $10,000 a year for three years to hire an education director. "He told us a lot about how to talk to children and how to make it interesting," said Clarkson. "And from then on, we always had an education director, and everyone took courses, and it was a very rigorous thing to do, but a wonderful program. I can remember that we used to have our little children all around, and then, standing over there listening, was Walter Chrysler. It was somewhat intimidating. I kept thinking, 'Am I well-enough informed?' He never interrupted and he always was very generous and polite and would say, 'You did a wonderful job.'"[7]

Chrysler organized an advisory committee, modeled after one at the Museum of Modern Art. The Chrysler Council was a group that grew into a fund-raising arm. Clarkson was involved with the group from the start. One of its first contributions was to make earphones available to museum patrons for self-guided tours.

The museum's art school was still in place when Chrysler arrived in Norfolk. Rita Marlier had been teaching sculpture and figure drawing there since 1968, when she'd moved to the area from Pittsburgh. She noted that Chrysler seemed to have mixed feelings about the school, which had been in operation for about a year and a half and emphasized pottery classes. On one hand, Chrysler appeared interested in the art school's potential. He wanted to enhance the painting classes and, for one semester, invited some New York painters to teach there. On the other hand, he didn't want to maintain it full-time, since it took money away from museum acquisitions. "No art school pays its own way," Marlier said. "Any art school is subsidized."[8]

Chrysler would ask Marlier to do occasional odd jobs for him at the museum. "For example, she said, "when somebody crashed into the wallpaper downstairs and left a hole, I got the job of matching that little piece of wallpaper so you wouldn't see it. And when he came in with the Velázquez painting, he wanted me to come over with acrylic paints because he had gotten a drapery to hang behind it for the unveiling—this huge velvet drapery with the painting hanging in front of it—and the wires of the painting were heavy picture-hanging wires, and they showed against the drape. So I went over with my paints and they had a fourteen-foot ladder so I could get up to the wire. I went up to the top of the wire. I matched the color.

"As soon as I touched the wire with the paintbrush all the alarms in the museum went off. There I am on top of a fourteen-foot ladder with all this paint over this rare Velázquez! And there are the guards running all around. The real danger was that I'd fall off the ladder into the painting."

In April 1973, the Selden House, where the Chrysler Museum school was located, was heavily damaged in a late-night fire. Arson investigators never discovered the cause of the blaze, which affected all three floors of the antebellum structure. A building across the street, part of which housed a bar called the Recovery Room, also was used for Marlier's drawing and sculpture studio, but there wasn't enough space there to compensate for what had been destroyed in the fire.

"Dr. Roper bought the Selden House and restored it, and it's beautiful," said Marlier. "People said, 'It's amazing what a new coat of paint and some good wood and a couple million dollars will do for a building.'"

12

SETTLING IN

Walter and Jean Chrysler purchased a handsome, 1890s-vintage townhouse at 735 Yarmouth Street, within walking (and viewing) distance of what Chrysler considered *his* museum. On most of the days he was in Norfolk, he would stroll over and either post himself at the staff entrance or wander around the galleries to oversee his collection's new home.

In New York, where he spent the majority of his time, he continued to wheel and deal for art, intent on filling gaps in what was steadily becoming the comprehensive, encyclopedic collection he had long envisioned. His preferred method for acquiring the more costly works continued to be trade. In order to fill chronological or stylistic gaps in his collection, Chrysler would barter with works by artists he believed were already overrepresented.

The art historian and Picasso biographer John Richardson, in his 2001 essay collection, *Sacred Monsters, Sacred Masters,* wrote, "[Jack] Tanzer could turn a minor Vlaminck into two Frank Stellas and, after a few more permutations, end up with a Rembrandt drawing," Richardson wrote. "He also had a knack of turning unsalable old masters into profitable assets. For instance, Tanzer knew that Walter Chrysler Jr.—a rogue whose excessive tax deductions for blatant fakes had been disallowed by the IRS—needed to acquire some respectable old masters on the cheap. And so he arranged for Chrysler to take a number of discredited paintings, which had been on Knoedler's books for fifty years or more at huge valuations, in exchange for one superb Cézanne."[1]

"One of the first things Walter wanted was a Velázquez, which was so rare," said Jack Tanzer. "It was really hard work, because I had to take pictures in exchange for these things, and then I'd have to sell all those pictures. But we managed to work it out where he got most of the pictures that he wanted and I was able to sell most of them. So it was somewhat profitable for the company."[2]

Beginning in late 1971, Chrysler was weeding out his collection, especially the paintings he'd acquired from a dealer who had sold Chrysler most of the proven forgeries from the Controversial Century exhibit. Chrysler would never tell exactly how he disposed of all of those pictures before he moved to Norfolk, but "even his staunchest detractors" in that city had no doubt that he had.[3] After that, Tanzer's work with Chrysler focused on deals for the museum. In the Chrysler's painting catalogue, if a picture's provenance is listed as Museum Art Exchange, E. V. Thaw, or Hirschl, it means that Tanzer brokered the trade; Chrysler did not pay cash for them. Chrysler was trading primarily to acquire nineteenth-century or Old Master paintings, with a very few moderns.

"He was getting rid of things," Tanzer said, "real good things. Some of them I think he should have kept: Picassos, etcetera. I sold a Picasso to Japan but got the museum great things that they needed. Unfortunately, some of them didn't arrive there until after he died; he gave a batch of them to his nephew in the will."

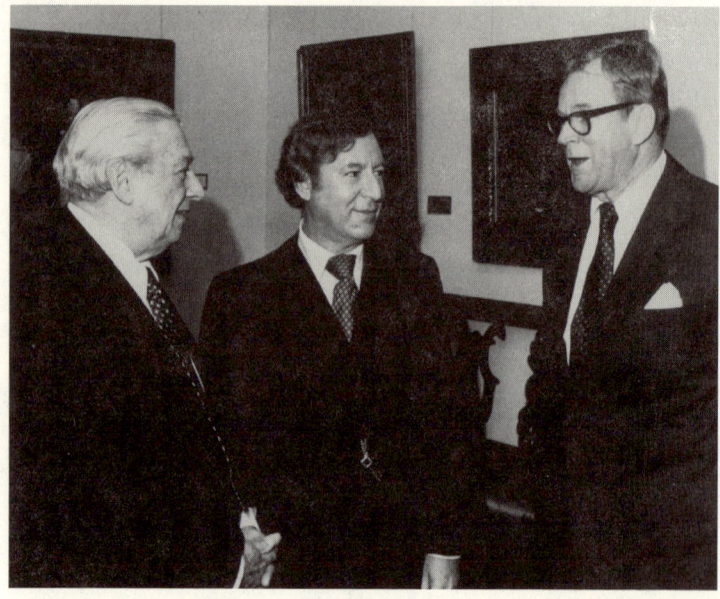

Left to right, Walter Chrysler, Jack Tanzer, and T. Lane Stokes. Tanzer was an art dealer who brokered many of the famous (and not always wise) trades Walter made to broaden his art collection. Stokes was Walter's friend and doctor, as well an influential member of the Chrysler Museum's board of directors. (Courtesy of the Chrysler Museum of Art, Norfolk, Va.)

Tanzer had donated his own pre-Colombian art collection to the Chrysler, and the museum honored him with a ceremony and his name on a plaque. He also donated a portrait of himself by Andy Warhol, which had been one of a set of four. Chrysler, said Tanzer, insisted he wanted only one. It was Chrysler who convinced Tanzer to cease being an independent dealer and join Knoedler's gallery, one of the oldest in America, right after it was purchased by Armand Hammer, the billionaire doctor, Occidental Oil CEO, entrepreneur, and art collector. During the fourteen years Tanzer was with Knoedler's, when Chrysler saw something he wanted or was looking for something, he'd call Tanzer and begin the machinations of a trade that Tanzer would have to convert into money in order to make the purchase.

"Walter and I were always in touch," Tanzer said. "When he saw something, he got excited about it. We'd have fights when I couldn't find a way to make an exchange. Thinking back, it was a lot of fun—it was a lot of aggravation, too, but I don't regret it. I had to get *Washington Crossing the Delaware,* a tough deal. I paid a fortune for that; Walter really wanted it because [the painter Albert] Bierstadt said it was his [Bingham's] greatest picture. The last major deal I made with him was the Delacroix. I got two Picassos in that deal, a Braque, a Cézanne—terrific things he gave up to get it. I would like to have seen them at the museum. All the dealers remember that one," Tanzer added, noting that he had to work with five different dealers to broker the trade. "Everybody made a lot of money, but it was a tough deal."

According to Eric Zafran, who would serve as chief curator at the Chrysler a few years later, Chrysler could make bad trades, too. He took Zafran to a New York warehouse to show him a Blue Period Picasso, a Braque, and other major paintings that were to be used in a trade for a Chinese Chippendale cabinet. "It seemed an unbalanced, whimsical deal to me, and it didn't happen," wrote Zafran. Nevertheless, Chrysler eventually traded the modern pictures for what Zafran believed was a mediocre group of Old Masters.[4]

"Sad to say, in this, as in so many other art judgments, he was mistaken," Zafran wrote. "He would not listen to art advice from anyone but his old cronies, who made out very well on the deals. As I came to realize, he had little money to spend and just loved to make deals for the sake of the deals, which meant trading off things he already had."

Tom Sokolowski thought Chrysler saw the trade as a game. "It was boring if you said, 'Here's an El Greco for $5 million.

Where's the check?'" he said. "Instead, it was, 'I'll sell you this chair, then you sell this chair to your nephew, who will then sell it for a Ferrari, and the Ferrari will then be sold back to Jack Tanzer, who will then give us the painting!'

"It meant weeks and months, sometimes, of all this kind of imbroglio." Sokolowski remembered when he and Tom Styron, the museum's American and contemporary art curator, had to select some things to be used in a trade. He, Styron, and Tanzer walked through the galleries together, and when Tanzer would say, "'Oh, that glass vase is really quite wonderful.' 'Oh, that's really an interesting sculpture,' the two curators knew: There's the list. And sure enough, when the trade came, what was on the list? The glass vase, the sculpture. We screamed and yelled, and I think at that point the whole deal did fall through. But he was so keen on having these things."

Sokolowski recalled an instance when Chrysler sent him to New York to see Tanzer about a painting, and Tanzer told Sokolowski to select from a couple of Chrysler's picks. Sokolowski chose a fifteenth-century painting by an anonymous artist titled *The Stigmatization of St. Francis*. Rather than quote a price, Sokolowski said, Tanzer introduced him to a jeweler from the Ritz in Boston. Then Tanzer opened a jewelry box and pulled out an enormous aquamarine and diamond brooch. The jeweler picked up the brooch, Sokolowski said, "like he was picking up a Coca-Cola can, and goes to the window. And he's assessing it and says, 'This isn't gem quality,' which I guess is the very best cut, but it was the next best."

The jeweler offered $25,000 for it. "I remember sitting there and thinking, what museum curator has to go and deal with a sleazy jeweler to trade a brooch for a fifteenth-century panel painting?" Sokolowski said. "The thing that was interesting about Walter was that probably other people do the same thing. But it's all behind closed doors, and a curator would never be party to it."

David Steadman said, "I used to weep when I was the director and I would go to other museums and see what Walter once owned," but Steadman understood that Chrysler had "decided he was going to put together a museum collection. He made a very conscious decision to do that."

"Walter was a character, you know," Tanzer said. "He was not easy to deal with. It's amazing I did so many things with him, but I liked him and I liked his wife. He was an intelligent man. He had this weird life he lived. I heard many stories. But, somehow or other, we stayed friends. Other people had fights with him. We had fights, too, but we'd get together again. Because he'd want something!"[5]

Tony Cacalano, a painter, had been writing freelance art criticism for the *Virginian-Pilot* when Chrysler's secretary called him to say that Chrysler admired his writing. Would he like to come over to the museum to see the collection?

While Chrysler showed him around, Cacalano recalled passing a gallery where several curators were struggling to free a painting from its frame. "It was probably three hundred to four hundred years old," Cacalano said, "a painting on wood panel, and they were afraid to pop it out." Chrysler said, "Tony, you're a painter," and suggested he help the other men. Cacalano casually pushed down on the panel, and out it came. "Everybody but Walter gasped. He said, 'I like the fact that you have a healthy disregard for priceless objects!'" Chrysler offered him a job on the spot, and Cacalano became an assistant curator and, later, the museum registrar.

Cacalano remembered that one of the first temporary exhibits at the new Chrysler Museum had nothing to do with art. The show, which opened in August 1971, was an elaborate celebration of the United States space program, on loan from the National Aeronautics and Space Administration. A centerpiece of the show was a moon rock. "You couldn't go anywhere near it without setting an alarm off," Cacalano said. "You had to unlock two keys and lift off this Plexiglas bulletproof dome from its pedestal. Every night the moon rock was taken out and put in a vault."

Early one morning, before the specimen was placed on display, one of the museum's carpenters placed a different rock under the dome. It was one he'd plucked from the parking lot of the Recovery Room, the popular saloon where some of the museum's art classes were taught. Just for fun, the carpenter and some of his coworkers drew up a plaque that looked exactly like the real one, but which identified the object as a genuine Ghent rock discovered on the ground outside the bar.

Cacalano had come in early that day. "As I walked in," he said, "I saw all these carpenters standing around, and they were goofing on the rock: 'Oh, that's a fantastic rock, fantastic!' I bent over it and read the plaque and started laughing. Just about then, Chrysler walked in, and he saw us all milling around the rock. He came over and bent down and put his hands on the tops of his knees and said, 'Isn't it beautiful? Just think. It's just fantastic! You fellows have a real treat, don't you?'

"And then he saw the plaque, and he went ballistic. He said, 'Where's the guard?' They found the poor guard, and Chrysler said, 'How did this happen?'" The guard told Chrysler he had been checking on an alarm that had gone off in another part of the museum, and he hadn't seen any of what the others had been up to.

Cacalano quoted Chrysler as saying, "My guards have to be able to be in two places at once. You're fired!" Willis Potter, the Chrysler's exhibit manager and designer who was one of the carpenters at that time, corroborated Cacalano's story. "[Chrysler] didn't have a sense of humor that day," Potter said. "That's when we realized—no more joking."[6]

Kirk Clarkson related a different consequence of Chrysler's tendency to arrive at the museum hours before it opened. One morning in 1972, she said, a few other docents came in and noticed a valuable painting was missing. "Everyone said, 'Where's the Matisse? Heavens! Has there been a burglary?'" she recalled. "But Walter had just gotten up early, and he'd taken it off the wall," Clarkson said. "He'd taken it to New York and traded it for a much better Matisse, which is the one we have now." Chrysler had traded the Matisse entitled *Vase of Gladioli* for another called *Bowl of Apples*.

"I understand that the board called him in, and they said, 'Walter, these paintings are not yours. You have given them to the City of Norfolk! We know they're just like your children but you cannot go and take anything off the wall without the permission of the board.' Clarkson said, with a laugh, "He was just upgrading!"

It was not an isolated incident. Over a period of about eight months, Chrysler exchanged a number of artworks displayed in the museum. The board let him know, in no uncertain terms, that it had veto power over changes in the collection. Chrysler, however, felt that his agreement with the city allowed him to make as many trades as he pleased.[7] In fact, the terms of the original agreement with Chrysler were specifically written to guard against what had happened. The agreement stated that Chrysler could only dispose of his objects in the museum with the trustees' approval—and vice versa.

But Chrysler insisted he needed the freedom to eliminate duplicates and fill gaps in the collection. His goal was simply to elevate the quality of the museum, he said, despite someone else's attachment to a particular work. He may have obtained that work specifically for a future trade, and since trades often involved acting quickly, he didn't want to be encumbered by "second-guessers," such as trustees, accessions committees—or docents. In anger, Chrysler stormed out and wrote Mason that he was going back to New York and that "the museum could run itself while he decided what his connection with it would be."

During his absence, Henry Clay Hofheimer hired a Sotheby Parke Bernet vice president to inspect the traded paintings and compare them with the originals under discussion. The auction house officer and an associate found the collection to have been neither diminished nor appreciated by the trades. The museum subsequently approved the trades but also resolved "that the current inventorying and cataloging of the collection . . . be expedited." What gave the board further ammunition were deeds Chrysler had given the City of Norfolk the previous year. Those deeds stated that Chrysler was giving a certain number of works, including the Matisse in question, to the museum with "the specific intent of the parties . . . that legal title to all of said paintings shall be vested in the Board of Trustees of the Chrysler Museum."[8]

Not surprisingly, Judge Parker was one of three trustees who filed a motion in Norfolk Circuit Court about the exchanges. Parker also accused Chrysler of moving his collection to Norfolk because his Cape Cod museum was "in financial difficulties and he was seeking shelter from the creditors."[9] He mentioned an art dealer who was suing the Provincetown museum for $18,750 and a Cleveland antique store that was seeking a temporary restraining order on the museum because of its failure to pay back a $23,559 loan, among other examples.

As Chrysler's absence stretched into months, Hofheimer was named the board's acting chief executive. Mason later wrote that he proposed that a committee visit Chrysler "and forge an arrangement that would allow him to return. I believed the task would be easy." The board approved, and Mason, Dr. Eugene F. Poutasse, and Phil Trapani flew to New York on November 1, 1972. They met for four hours with Chrysler and Frank Vanderlip in Chrysler's Upper East Side apartment. The group dined on a catered lunch of hamburgers and beer.

They came to an agreement that the art Chrysler had brought to Norfolk would be separated into two categories. One would be a special "permanent collection," not to be removed without the approval of the museum's accessions committee and board of trustees. All the other art objects from the Provincetown museum would be available for Chrysler to trade or sell as he chose, "for the purpose of improving the Chrysler Museum's collection." Chrysler also agreed to meet regularly and work closely with the accessions committee to obtain their advice for any future trades or transactions."

While Poutasse and Trapani left to fly back to Norfolk, Mason, who was planning to stay in New York to see a show, lingered in the apartment to chat with Chrysler. Chrysler told Mason that Vanderlip was his oldest friend and had been the best man at Chrysler's first wedding. Mason hadn't known that Jean Outland was Chrysler's second wife.

"He must have sensed my surprise," Mason wrote. "Suddenly he erupted. 'While I'll be forever grateful to you, Bob, for understanding from the first what I'm trying to accomplish, the rest of your board are a bunch of damn fools cutting their throats by interfering with everything I undertake to benefit them and the City of Norfolk. For Christ's sake! I have just one objective for the rest of my life, which won't last long: no male member of my family since God knows when has lived past 66 and I'm pushing that. I intend to build a museum that damn well could become the final monument to the Chrysler name, outliving the company my father founded . . . and the fortune he built and passed on. I'm not leaving a penny to Jean—not one cent . . . I'm estranged from what few next-generation relatives I have. My estate is willed to the Chrysler Museum. But if your stupid board won't cooperate, my will is mine for changing!' I was stunned," Mason added. "But Frank Vanderlip, I noticed, did not seem to be impressed by the tantrum."[10]

By this time, word of the ongoing series of conflicts at the Chrysler had spread beyond the borders of Hampton Roads. In fact, members of Richmond's art community had taken to calling it "The Crisis Museum."[11] Despite the moon rock incident, Willis Potter's memories of those early years at the Chrysler were mostly positive. He had come to the museum while he was an art student majoring in graphic design at Norfolk State College. Inquiring about a summer job, he was hired to work in the maintenance shop, where the exhibits were built. Potter was thrilled to be able to handle original works of art. When Chrysler discovered that Potter wanted to be an artist and study in New York, he put him on the crew that made frequent trips to that city to bring warehoused art down for shows.

Potter had the opportunity to meet artists and art dealers. Chrysler often suggested Potter visit museums while he was in Manhattan; sometimes he gave the younger man personal advice. "He wouldn't ask about me," Potter recalled, "he would *tell* me about me! I thank him for that. It was great. But Mr. Chrysler was a tough man. Not everyone could deal with his personality. Sometimes I wouldn't wish him on my worst enemy. He was a difficult person to work with because he was used to having things his way. At the same time, he also liked a good fight. If you couldn't fight, you might as well pack up. He had to get to know you, to feel comfortable with you, and he had to feel you were worth even dealing with."

Potter noticed that Chrysler changed when he was in New York. At the museum, everyone called him "Mr. Chrysler," but in New York, it was "Walter." "Once, when we had to go to Park Avenue, he said, 'Oh, Potter, that's where the rich people stay!' And I'm thinking, *rich people?* How does he see himself? I thought *he* was a rich person! When he was here, he was playing a role. But he was just a regular guy who was born rich."

During his trips to New York, Potter often had to pick artwork up from one of Chrysler's warehouses. He remembered one in SoHo, one on Sixty-first Street, and another at Eighty-fourth Street and Amsterdam Avenue. "He would have rooms about sixteen by twelve feet with about ten-foot ceilings with cages or storage rooms," Potter said. "We had paintings separated by cardboard. He had a person in New York who handled the cataloging of the collection. He knew what was in the stacks and the registrar in New York knew."

Although Potter's recollection of Chrysler's demeanor at the museum in Norfolk was "all business," there were times when he would loosen up and mimic his father's penchant for practical jokes. Julie Dalton remembered one he played on her. She had told him there was going to be a meeting of women from the Garden Club in the Chrysler Museum's auditorium. She asked if he would please select a special, appropriately themed picture for the occasion to be hung at the entrance. Chrysler agreed.

"I thought he'd put some flower paintings out there," said Dalton. Instead, the clubwomen were shocked to discover Tintoretto's *Allegorical Figure of Spring,* an extravagantly voluptuous reclining female, one of her plump breasts spilling out of her dress and a bare leg suggestively propped up against a tree. "That was his sense of humor," said Dalton, laughing. "It was wonderful!"

As he did in Provincetown, Chrysler obsessed about the tiniest detail at the Norfolk museum. "He had this habit when we were setting up an exhibit," Potter remembered. "He'd get a folding chair and sit right in the middle of the gallery. He'd direct you and watch you work. If you were a nervous person, it would be too much pressure. I just learned to ignore him."

Decorative arts curator Mark Clark recalled that Chrysler "promised he wouldn't interfere with my work," but that when Clark displayed objects, Chrysler "always had to move it a hair, just to put his fingers on it. It used to make me furious. He was one of those micromanagers."

Chrysler's nit-picking wasn't reserved for museum displays, as Kenneth M. Beam found out. Beam, who was museum administrator in the late 1970s, was walking through a gallery one day when he was stopped by Chrysler. "You're the administrator of a major museum. You shouldn't be out here without your coat on!" Chrysler said. "Walter was a real down-and-dirty detail person," Beam added. "He cared as much about what the guards wore as he cared about anything else."[12]

About his own attire he seemed less concerned. Tom Sokolowski recalled that the first time he saw Chrysler he had no idea who he was. "I started up in the summer and heard that Walter was away for a month or two. And then I said to someone, 'I thought Mr. Chrysler was going to be back.' And they said, 'Oh, Walter is back. You probably see him when you come in, in the mornings at the back door. He's a big guy with a big stomach wearing a bowling shirt.'"

"I said, 'Oh, God! I thought he was some sort of delivery man or something,' because he would sit there, squatting on a chair," Sokolowski said. "He had funny things about wanting to know when people came in and if they were earning their money."

13

BIG CHANGES

Pablo Picasso died on April 8, 1973. Two months later, the Chrysler became the first American museum to mount a posthumous show of his work. The exhibit consisted of twenty paintings and sculptures, four of the paintings from Walter Chrysler's collection, and the others on loan from other institutions, including the Museum of Modern Art.

Ann Vernon, an unemployed Williamsburg art teacher, visited the show. When she returned home, Vernon wrote a letter to the Chrysler addressed "To Whom It May Concern." In it, she praised the museum and the exhibit but suggested it could stand some improvements, including better labels for the artwork and a tour guide. "Nothing like chutzpah!" Vernon said. "Within a week, I had a telephone call from Capt. Wahlig, [the] administrator at the time, and he said, 'Mr. Chrysler would like to meet you.' No letter or anything. Just a telephone call—a summons!"[1]

As soon as they met, Chrysler hired Vernon as director of education. Her staff consisted of "about five faithful volunteers who had been with the museum when it was the Norfolk Museum of Arts and Sciences," Vernon said. Under her leadership, the education department's pool of volunteers would climb to about twenty times that number. These volunteers were made up of wealthy, sophisticated, educated, and well-traveled women, said Vernon. She said that Chrysler valued the education department, and not just because the museum needed to have one to be eligible for city, state, and federal funding. "He truly believed in the mission of educating young people," she said.

In February 1975, Walter Chrysler bestowed a rare treasure on the Chrysler Museum and the City of Norfolk: the painting *Saint Phillipe* by Georges de la Tour, a relatively unknown seventeenth-century French artist. De la Tour, like Vermeer, had produced only a small number of pictures; he is most noted for subjects in dark rooms illuminated only by the glow of candlelight. At the time of Chrysler's acquisition, for which he traded several paintings valued at about $1.4 million, only six de la Tours were owned by American museums; the National Gallery had paid a reported $6 million for the one in its collection. The gift was the most valuable single painting given to the city by Chrysler up to that point.[2]

A month later, Chrysler's sister Bernice Garbisch and her husband, Col. Edgar Garbisch, donated forty-eight eighteenth- and nineteenth-century naïve American paintings. Sixteen of the forty-eight were outright gifts; the rest came on extended loan but would eventually become the museum's property. The estimated value of the group was $1 million. The Garbisches' entire collection, acquired over a period of thirty-one years, was the most comprehensive of its kind in the world. They had made similar gifts to other museums, including the National Gallery, the Metropolitan, and the Whitney. These additions were especially welcome to the Chrysler because they filled a gap in its American art collection.[3]

That year was a busy one for the Chrysler Museum in many ways. While Walter Chrysler's true loves were indisputably art and the museum, he had never lost his attraction to the theater. In July, more than twenty years after his Broadway producer days, he and the director of the Barter Theater announced that the famed Abingdon, Virginia, playhouse would make the Chrysler Museum its winter home. The Barter, which was the official state theater of Virginia, was founded during the Depression, and on its stage had appeared such stars as Patricia Neal, Gregory Peck, and Ernest Borgnine. Fund-raising soon began at the Chrysler as a sum of $50,000 would be needed to launch the Barter's first season.[4]

Bringing the Barter to the Chrysler Museum, like virtually everything Chrysler did, proved controversial. The local Actors' Theater, which had been using the museum's auditorium for its productions, had to move because it would not have been able to survive without a winter season. And although the Actors' Theater director, G. F. (Gerry) Rowe, insisted he was in favor of the Barter's coming because it would raise the bar for all theater in the area, he was pessimistic that local audiences could support the Barter's planned five or six performances a week of the same production.

Chrysler, however, saw the Barter's arrival as another sign that Norfolk would one day become a complete center for the visual and performing arts.[5] As it turned out, the theater's first season at the museum would be its only one. Even attendance averaging more than two-thirds capacity for each performance couldn't compensate for the lack of public contributions and reduction of government grants.[6]

Other amenities were added to the museum in this period as well. A music listening room was installed, where visitors could take advantage of a free audio system providing access to radio, a phonograph, and a tape recorder. Headphones were offered at the reception desk, and specific recordings were featured at scheduled times.

Tony Cacalano remembered an innovation designed to lure more people into the museum and raise money. During the summer of 1975, he and the museum's public relations director organized "Monday Nights at the Chrysler."[7] Their idea was to put on a series of programs with music, film, and lectures every week for a one-dollar admission fee. Programs and events designed to draw community members into museum buildings and increase membership, have become ubiquitous as government funding declines.

Also in 1975, Gaston Lachaise's anatomically correct statue *Man* was placed in the museum's parking lot. The well-endowed nude, which had caused such a stir outside Walter and Peggy Chrysler's Great Neck home thirty-seven years earlier, was about to do it again. At a meeting, a couple of Norfolk city councilmen declared the statue obscene. One of them suggested that funding for the museum be withheld until the bronze giant was removed.

Common sense came in the person of City Attorney Trapani, who helped convince his colleagues there was nothing offensive about the statue.[8] The *Virginian-Pilot* had harsher words for the priggish councilmen: "This is a timely reminder that the seamier side of Puritanism is alive in Norfolk."[9]

Controversies about art inside the museum were percolating as well. Later that year, another Norfolk councilman commented on the large number of displayed artworks still marked "on loan from Walter P. Chrysler Jr." Referring to the remark in a lecture to the Tidewater Artists Association, Chrysler said that some of those labels would be replaced with ones marked "gift of" as soon as the Internal Revenue Service allowed them as tax deductions.

Chrysler complained that more money was needed to

operate the museum and to acquire new works but that the funds would have to be provided without political strings attached if the institution was to be considered valid. This, he said, had so far been denied him.[10] Nonetheless, he soon announced he was giving the museum twenty-two masterpieces. In an interview, Chrysler said he had chosen to make the gifts at that time to recognize Norfolk's support of cultural development. But it was revealed shortly thereafter that the museum was already the official owner of the works and had been since 1971. Chrysler hastily informed Mayor Irvine B. Hill that, within the next two years, he would make bona fide gifts to the museum of a sculpture and fifteen important paintings.[11] To be sure, the incident raised eyebrows.

On March 1 of America's bicentennial year, a new wing opened to the public at the Chrysler Museum. Comprising twenty galleries, the two-story addition more than doubled the museum's exhibit space. The $1.5-million project was paid for by the City of Norfolk as part of its original agreement with Chrysler in 1971 when he moved his collection from Provincetown.

The Chrysler's chief curator at that time was Dennis Anderson, who left the following year to work on his doctorate in New York. Anderson was replaced by Dr. Eric Zafran, who came to the Chrysler from the European Painting Department at the Metropolitan Museum of Art. Zafran seemed glad to get away from the Met, which he described to a reporter as a huge bureaucracy. The Chrysler seemed a lot less formal.

"We can avoid a lot of that red tape," Zafran said in a newspaper interview, "just because we're all on a first-name basis." Acknowledging his youth (he was thirty at the time) and the relatively young staff members he would be supervising,

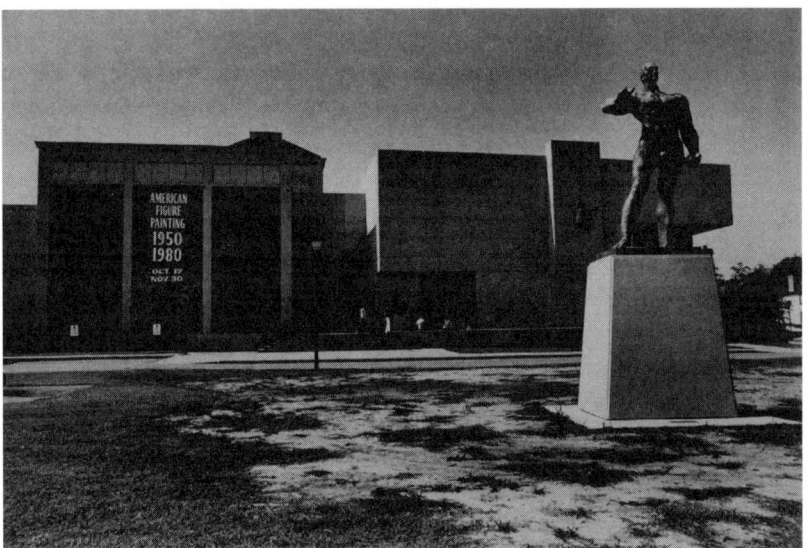

The Chrysler Museum of Art's Centennial Wing, 1980. View of the museum while Lachaise's *Man* was still standing outdoors, outraging city councilman and one irate hammer-wielding citizen. (Courtesy of the Chrysler Museum of Art, Norfolk, Va.; photograph by Brooks Johnson.)

Zafran looked to the future. "We'll learn from doing," he said, "and we have Mr. Chrysler to guide us."[12]

Looking back on his experiences, Zafran—now curator of American and European painting and sculpture at the Wadsworth Atheneum in Hartford, Connecticut—admitted that reality soon quashed that initial optimism. "Walter Chrysler needed an art historian to help professionalize the museum," he explained, "and offered me the job of chief curator, which seemed like a great opportunity to work with a remarkable, if uneven, collection."

Zafran was disappointed to discover, however, that Chrysler maintained so much control over the museum that instead of functioning as chief curator, his duties ended up being the production of catalogues for paintings and drawings in the European collection. Just before Zafran arrived, he wrote, Chrysler had been buying a lot of American art for the museum's new wing. Then he acquired "a mixed group" of Old Masters, decorative arts, and an early Italian painting, but Zafran could not recall "a truly great addition" to the collection during his tenure.[13]

In February 1976, the *New York Times* art critic Hilton Kramer was invited to Norfolk to judge the Irene Leache annual painting competition and show. In an article in *M* magazine, Kramer later mentioned that brief Norfolk stay, during which he became the butt of another of Walter Chrysler's practical jokes. "The museum had lent us a space for our arduous task—many hours looking at a lot of bad painting," Kramer wrote. "Chrysler came in, introduced himself and said that if I weren't engaged, there was to be a dinner of some sort at the museum that night, and that he'd be happy to have me join the party as his guest. As the dinner came to an end, I realized that Chrysler had stood to announce how pleased he was to present the speaker of the evening, namely myself. Well, I thought, if this is the name of the game, I can play too. So I rose, said, 'Thank you,' and sat down. Chrysler had a tantrum and never spoke to me again."[14] And, as was later apparent, Kramer never forgot, nor completely forgave, his host.

In November 1976, Chrysler suggested for the first time that he was considering retiring as director of the museum. He'd been in the post without pay for several years; he was sixty-seven years old and felt, he said, that active management should be reserved for those sixty-five and younger. His rationale for staying in the position as long as he had was that he wanted to see the museum's new wing completed.

In an article about Chrysler's decision to step down, the *Virginian-Pilot* published words that would seem prophetic twelve years later: "While he has never gone on record with the intention of settling the total collection on the museum, it is not too difficult to read between the lines of his statements about intending to make it a great institution to understand that only a catastrophe would avert that eventuality."[15]

Chrysler's successor as director, it was generally believed, would surely be the forty-three-year-old administrator hired two months earlier, Mario Amaya.[16] Jack Tanzer recalled being asked his advice when Amaya was under consideration. The dealer knew that Amaya was a recognized expert on modern art. He also suspected, he said, that there would be problems.

"They called me, and I said, 'He's a good director, he'll be fine—BUT!'"[17]

14

OH! MARIO!

As expected, on the first day of 1977 the board of trustees unanimously voted to promote Mario Amaya from administrator to interim director. The "interim" was added at Walter Chrysler's insistence after he expressed surprise at the board's decision, as well as a reluctance to officially step down as he had promised. The qualifier was soon dropped, however.[1] As it turned out, Amaya's tenure at the Chrysler was relatively brief, but when former colleagues hear his name, each has a story to tell. Many look back with amusement, if not affection, on the exciting and volatile period they call "the Mario era."

Amaya, a Brooklyn, New York, native and Brooklyn College alumnus, had been an art critic for a string of impressive periodicals in this country and abroad. His social circle consisted of the jet set and the international modern art in-crowd. Before coming to Virginia, he'd been director of the New York Cultural Center, where he curated a series of groundbreaking shows. After the center closed, Amaya was in Richmond, interviewing for a curatorial job at the Virginia Museum, when he met Walter Chrysler.[2]

A photograph from the period shows Amaya looking movie-star handsome and dressed impeccably. Describing himself as an "activator," he compared the job of museum director with being a Ziegfeld.[3] "I'm a showman," he said. "A catalyst. I make things happen." He did not misrepresent himself.

Ticking off some of his prior accomplishments, Amaya said he'd introduced John Lennon to Yoko Ono, was a founding editor of *Art and Artists* magazine, and had been commissioned to write the first definitive book on Pop Art. He knew all the major players of the genre including, and especially, its reigning king: Andy Warhol. In fact, Amaya had happened to be visiting Warhol at his studio, the Factory, the day Warhol was shot by Valerie Solanas. Amaya was grazed during the shooting spree, suffering a flesh wound a half-inch from his spine. Warhol spent two months in the hospital recovering from his critical injuries, but Amaya, after an emergency-room patch-up, was released and proceeded with his evening dinner plans.

"I loved Mario Amaya," Ann Vernon said. "Mario was over the top, flamboyant, and knew *everybody*. You'd turn around and, between Mario and Walter, here would come Robert Mapplethorpe; there would be Sir John Pope-Hennessy. This place absolutely sizzled! I must say, nobody was observing the rules very much, but we were all having the most marvelous time.

"Mario and Walter would have screaming matches, and my office was just down the hall from Walter's," Vernon said. "It was as if the air-conditioning ducts would send their words, and they'd drop over my desk, cartoon form. You could see them! You just put your fingers in your ears."

Judith (Riley) Dressel, the museum's registrar in 1977, recalled that Amaya "would stand in his fabulous handmade suits, and he would have temper tantrums. He was jumping up and down in the hall, literally, and his face would turn red. He had this Cuban temper."[4]

Kenneth Beam concurred. "One minute he'd be yelling and screaming and running down the halls. Other times he'd be pretty calm. But you'd never know. He'd yell and scream if the weather went bad. Mario was a genius in his own way," he added. "But sometimes you don't want to be around geniuses."

Mike Goodwin, the official museum photographer at the time, remembers a conversation he had with Chrysler about Amaya. "I said to Walter, 'I figured something out. You hired Mario to make you look good because you were getting so much crap from everybody in the city and on the board. So you hire Mario and you come off looking like a choir boy.' Walter's just sitting there, jingling his keys, and he looks at me and says, 'Kid, you're a lot smarter than I've been giving you credit for.'"[5]

Brooks Johnson became the museum's photographer in December 1977. In 1980, he was appointed curator but still maintained his photographic duties. "Within a year of my coming here, we got a gallery for photography," he said. "Mario was the one responsible for applying for a grant and getting the gallery. I worked with the chief curator on the first three shows and then after that took it and ran with it and was able to raise money to make it go. I was the museum photographer in the daytime and in the evenings the curator. It was a pretty busy time."[6]

Johnson credits Amaya's friendship with the *enfant terrible* photographer Mapplethorpe for the Chrysler's 1978 exhibition of his work, the first in a series of important photography shows. "I made the copy photographs for the catalogue," Johnson said. "That catalogue and that exhibition were both Mapplethorpe's first—his first museum show; his first catalogue.

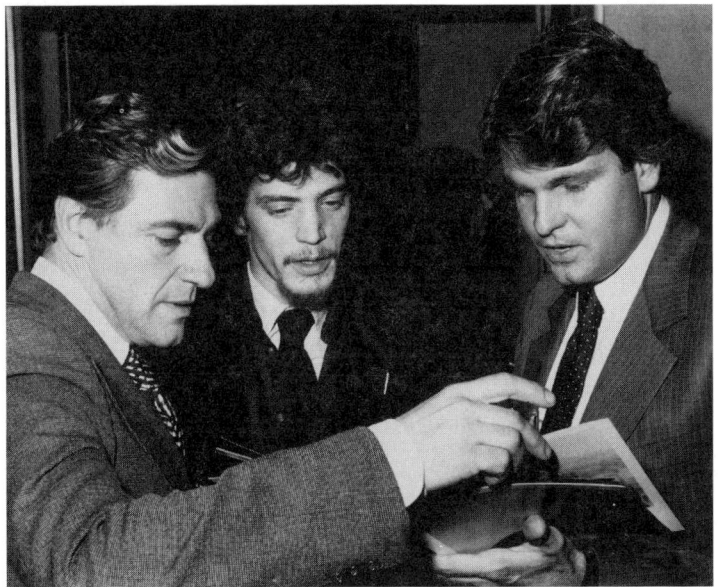

Left to right, Chrysler Museum director Mario Amaya, bad-boy photographer Robert Mapplethorpe, the author, and James Witt, on the occasion of Mapplethorpe's first museum show, which took place at the Chrysler in 1978. (Courtesy of the Chrysler Museum of Art, Norfolk, Va.; photograph by Brooks Johnson.)

"In the catalogue, we published one of the photos that Dennis Barrie was indicted on [charged with obscenity] in Cincinnati years later," he said. "Because of Chrysler and Mario, all these people were always dropping in, like Hockney and Rosenquist. Eartha Kitt came in. Vincent Price came in. I was making pictures of all these people," Johnson said. "It was a golden era, in a certain sense."

Amaya was a boon to the museum in more tangible ways as well. Under his leadership, the Chrysler received its first grant money, twice from the Virginia Commission of the Arts and Humanities and other funding from state and federal budgets.[7] And Amaya personally enhanced the museum's holdings by donating an original Man Ray and a collection of art books, drawings, and prints.

When Amaya's imminent departure from the Chrysler was reported in the press, the reason given was that he planned a six-month sabbatical in order to write and publish a federally funded catalogue for the museum. He was quoted as saying that he wasn't sure he'd return. "Everybody knew that Mario didn't like the town," Beam said. "He felt it was provincial. If they didn't like what he was doing, it was because they were small-minded provincial people. They didn't understand. After a couple years people got tired of that."

Rumors that Amaya was forced to leave were hinted at in a *Virginian-Pilot* article citing vague "conflicts with the board." Coworkers suggested less elevated reasons, including run-ins with the police for offenses such as drunken driving and public indecency. Chrysler insisted to the press that Amaya would be welcome to renegotiate his contract if he so desired, but that he "is so well qualified he may not want to come back to Norfolk."[8] Amaya never did return. Just eight years later, at the age of fifty-two, he died in London of AIDS-related illnesses.[9]

In January 1977, Mark A. Clark of Dayton, Ohio, was hired as curator of decorative arts. "My first meeting with Walter was in Dayton," Clark said. "I was curator and registrar at the Dayton Art Institute. Walter pestered me for a long time to come down," Clark said. "'I have a real museum and I need help.' So I came out to take a look and said, 'Oh my God, you do need help! This place is a mess.' There was stuff all over the place. He didn't know what he had. Nothing was recorded."

Clark visited one of Chrysler's warehouses. "I remember there was a *Head of Christ* by Rouault, an oil on paper mounted on board, or something. And there was a mop bucket right next to it, and they'd been slopping mop water all over it." Clark said that his first order of business was to create a written record of the collection. "Eventually I got things cleaned up and got more help," he said. "But you could never settle Walter down. That's why we got things down on paper so he couldn't take them back."

For the excellent Art Nouveau furniture collection, Clark said, "we raised money by deaccessioning to buy other things. We started bringing in experts in the field, three of them. Nothing was ever sold without three experts looking at it, and if they all agreed, it went. If any disagreed, it stayed."

Clark recalled the last time he saw Chrysler. "He came to the museum, to the back door. He brought me some dumb spoon that he'd gotten during lunch, and he got mad at me because I didn't want it. I said, 'Walter, that's not good enough for the collection.' And he just blew up."

In the fall of 1977, the City of Norfolk demonstrated its appreciation for the man who had brought excitement and art-world glamour to town. Mayor Vincent J. Thomas announced that September 27 was "Walter P. Chrysler Day." The proclamation presented at that evening's city council meeting cited Chrysler's cultural contributions to Norfolk. Thomas added from the dais that the museum had become one of the country's finest thanks to Chrysler's direction.[10]

By the end of that year, a *Town and Country* magazine article expressed surprise at the quality of the Chrysler Museum in a city as "uninspired" as Norfolk. It condemned the museum's architecture as "a hodgepodge of bastard Renaissance and Berlin Wall" and criticized the city's "lethargic community" for having taken seven years to figure out "that it is sitting on a gold mine and a treasure trove of art."

At sixty-eight, Chrysler was "a Friar Tuck with delicate features, keener eyes and a sharper tongue," the magazine reported, "who revealed that he was a simple guy who enjoyed eating his dinner on a tray in front of the television. 'When in Norfolk I live for my work,'" he was quoted as saying. "There's my private life and my public life." He added, enigmatically: "I plan to have two private lives one of these days!"

During the interview, the reporter and Chrysler strolled through the museum and paused at an Andy Warhol painting. "Andy's brilliant," Chrysler said. "A great artist, a humorist and innovator. I think of him as the Samuel Johnson of his generation!" A week after the interview, the same *Town and Country* reporter had lunch with Warhol and told him of Chrysler's complimentary words. "Gee, wow, isn't that just great!" replied Warhol, who then echoed a previously noted comparison: "I really dig Walter," he said. "He always makes me think of Santa Claus."[11]

Robert Indiana, another Pop Art superstar, came to the Chrysler in December 1977 for an important retrospective of his work. Indiana's most widely recognized piece is his *LOVE* painting, which was later reproduced on a U.S. postage stamp. The very popular show featured Indiana's costumes for a Gertrude Stein/Virgil Thompson opera, as well as his prints, paintings, and theater designs.

A much less publicized happening transformed Jean Chrysler's already impressive art library into the top art reference collection in the South and one of the ten most important in the nation. It was the purchase of the M. Knoedler & Co., Ltd., art reference library in London, then worth an estimated $500,000. The library contained a wealth of materials, including books, museum and gallery catalogues, and newspaper clip files. Touted as another gift from Walter Chrysler, the deal was brokered by Jack Tanzer.

Despite this tremendous addition to her collection, Jean

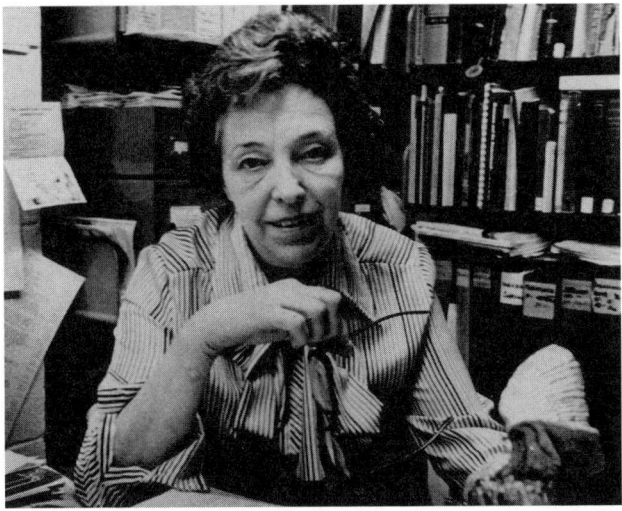

Jean Chrysler in the art library she struggled to maintain in an old school administration building in Norfolk. Several years after Jean's death, the library, which bears her name, was installed within the museum's walls. (Courtesy of the Chrysler Museum of Art, Norfolk, Va.)

Chrysler was exasperated. She told the *Ledger-Star* that even before the arrival of the Knoedler additions, the library was still packed in crates and piled in stacks on the City Hall Avenue School Administration Building's fifth floor. Valuable texts were exposed to leaky windows in that old building. Jean pointed to examples of unsalvageable casualties from a recent storm. She said the Knoedler collection would probably be left in a New York storage facility until enough money could be raised and matched by a challenge grant from the federal government to build a proper library space. Fund-raising events were in the works, including a Tidewater Ballet benefit, a carnival, a concert series—even the sale of museum tote bags—but they couldn't come too soon for the head librarian.[12]

One such fund-raiser was an April 1978 bus trip to New York from Norfolk to see a show of Chrysler Museum paintings exhibited at the renowned Wildenstein Galleries. A substantial amount of money was raised, but the real profits of the show came in the form of glowing reviews of the Chrysler's treasures from the art capital of the world.

In October, a $45,000 challenge grant was awarded the Chrysler Museum by the National Endowment for the Humanities toward the construction of the art library. The challenge was to the public, which would bear the responsibility of matching the NEH funds, three to one.

In early 1979, following the announcement of Mario Amaya's permanent "sabbatical," a new director was hired for the Chrysler Museum. Richard J. Wattenmaker, a Philadelphia native and one-time director of the Rutgers University Art Gallery, had been chief curator of Toronto's Art Gallery of Ontario. Lane Stokes, chairman of the Chrysler's board of trustees, declined to tell the press how many other candidates had been considered or what prompted Wattenmaker's selection, but a press release referred to his deep involvement in the Toronto museum's new $25-million building complex.[13]

As it happened, Wattenmaker's tenure at the Chrysler would be even briefer than Amaya's, lasting only ten months. When the end came, Stokes described Wattenmaker's resignation as "sort of a mutual agreement" between him and the board. Stokes's written statement to the museum staff, while praising Wattenmaker for his contributions, also granted that "his philosophies were not in full accord with the immediate needs of the Chrysler Museum and the board at this time," and that the director had agreed to remain in his position until a successor was hired. Stokes said Wattenmaker had advanced the museum toward its goal of professionalism, citing his renovation of fourteen galleries. Wattenmaker, however, said that he could not recommend the museum for accreditation.[14]

In February 1979, the Virginia State Senate unanimously approved a resolution honoring Walter Chrysler. The document acknowledged him as a "benefactor of the Commonwealth and a benefactor for the generations yet unborn" who made the Chrysler Museum "one of the finest in the country." Norfolk senator Stanley C. Walker introduced Chrysler to his fellow lawmakers and described his coming to Norfolk as "like a breath of fresh air across Eastern Virginia." In a brief statement, Chrysler demurred, saying that his wife had been vital to his decision to bring his collection to Norfolk and "should be honored today instead of me."[15]

15

The Lion Declawed

In July 1980, David Wilton Steadman was named the Chrysler Museum's third professional director. Steadman, forty-three, arrived in Norfolk with an impressive list of credentials: He had been director of the Galleries of the Claremont Colleges in Southern California as well as a professor of art at Pomona College. He also had been a research curator of the Norton Simon Museum in Pasadena, a collection with some similarities to the Chrysler's.

Steadman's arrival marked a turning point for the museum. Walter Chrysler, who had been president of the board, became chairman. The chairman, Dr. T. Lane Stokes, was elected president. "The swap underlines with a double stroke the decreasing role of Chrysler in the museum's day-to-day operation," the *Virginian-Pilot* reported.[1] The position of chairman, according to the museum board's bylaws, was mostly honorary—he ran the board meetings.

By all accounts, the museum had been in a state of flux for the two years since Mario Amaya left. Membership had leveled off, visitor numbers were low, and firings, layoffs, and resignations were commonplace. Despite that, three museum

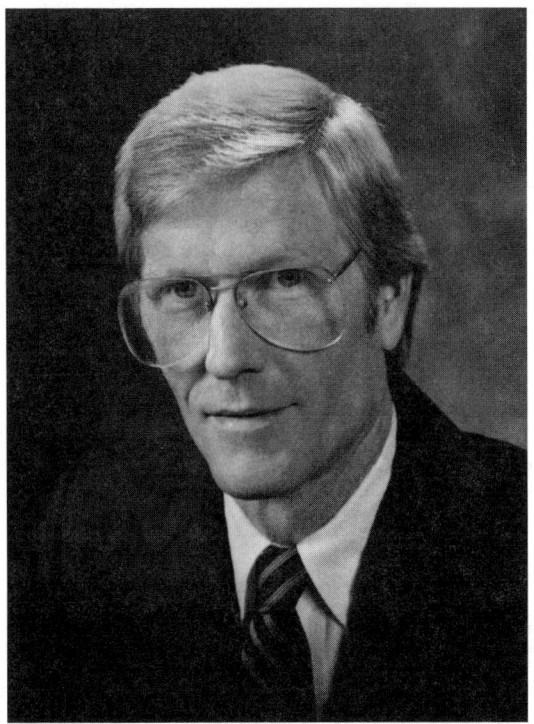

David Wilton Steadman, 1980. Steadman was director of the Chrysler Museum from 1980 to 1989, overseeing the most dramatic architectural changes in the museum, as well as its accreditation by the American Association of Museums. (Courtesy of the Chrysler Museum of Art, Norfolk, Va.; photograph by Wayne Book Photographs.)

experts invited by Stokes to assess the collection praised it as "one of the most outstanding groups of major pictures in the country."[2] Steadman's leadership would prove crucial, taking the Chrysler at last to full accreditation by the American Association of Museums.

"The first time I met Walter was when I was being interviewed," said Steadman. "I got a letter from Tommy Willcox, who was chairman of the search committee, saying that Irving Lavin, of the Institute for Advanced Study in Princeton, had recommended me to them. He went on to say that the board had commissioned a report from [Sherman] Lee in Cleveland and Evan Turner, who was then in Chapel Hill. "Evan is an old friend, and I called him and said, 'Should I even talk to these people? Their reputation is that this is the worst museum in the country.' It was a shambles at that point."

Turner advised Steadman to go to Norfolk for the interview anyway. On his second interview, Steadman insisted upon meeting Chrysler. "Walter and I met in this kind of deserted upstairs director's office," Steadman said. "We sat down, and he said, 'I understand that you're from Hawaii.' And he asked the classic southern question, 'Who was your mother's family?' I told him, and he said, 'Which one?'

"I said, 'Well, my grandfather was Clarence Cook,' and he said, 'Oh my God! I remember when my mother and I were on a trip to the Orient in 1929, and we stopped in Honolulu for a week. Your grandfather and grandmother had us up for lunch! After lunch your grandfather took me on a tour of his garden. At which point Walter proceeded to give me a twenty-minute description of my grandfather's garden," Steadman said. "We got through all that, and then we talked about art. Well, the upshot of this whole thing was that Walter tended to talk quite freely to me from then on."

As had so many before him, Steadman found Chrysler "a very complex man," who could be "absolutely charming beyond belief, an absolute son of a bitch," and "fairly manipulative. But at least in his relationship with me it was always reasonably straightforward. And so, throughout those years I was there, I always had a decent working relationship with him."

Steadman addressed the museum's previous failures to

achieve accreditation from the American Association of Museums (AAM). Among the reasons cited in a report by the AAM were inadequate fire protection and storage space. The AAM also urged the Chrysler's board to have its own charter of incorporation. At the time, the museum was still legally under the auspices of the Norfolk Society of Arts, which dated back to the founding of the Norfolk Museum of Arts and Sciences. Steadman said that the board used the AAM report as a "blueprint" of how to professionalize the museum. Richard Wattenmaker's role in that transformation was critical. He went through the list and tried to make the changes, such as providing decent storage, improving the organization of the museum, and changing the nature of the board, said Steadman.[3]

"The key player in all of that was Lane Stokes," Steadman said. "Without Lane none of this would have taken place. Lane was very smart, very shrewd. He could be very diplomatic, knew Walter backwards and forwards and knew how to work with people." Stokes also knew him inside and out—he was Chrysler's doctor.

"I had several long talks with Lane when I was there for interviews," Steadman said. "There was very little money to buy [art]. The only painting that Walter bought while I was there—the main one—was the [Filippino] Lippi. The only outright purchase we made was the Tissot, and, for that, we just took money from everywhere to come up with the funds. When I look back on it now, it was ludicrously cheap, but at the time it was expensive."

Tom Sokolowski called the Tissot purchase "a sort of hallmark. Walter wanted it, and David Steadman wanted a big highfalutin' thing in his early years in the museum. It was a very nice picture, but we pushed the market up so high it was ridiculous. It's not worth what the museum paid for it. There was a big to-do made about it, and I remember David

Steadman saying, 'This is the single most important . . .' And I remember saying, 'David, what are you going to say when we get a Raphael? Only one thing can be "the single most important!"'"

"As Walter got older, the money was getting fairly tight, and that was difficult," Sokolowski said. "But, for example, the museum owns the last major work by Gian Lorenzo Bernini, carved by Bernini's hand [*Bust of the Risen Savior*]. He bought it as seventeenth-century French, but it's an extraordinary piece of sculpture. No one at the time would have bought it. Walter wanted it because it was big and blousy. He took a chance on it because he liked its flashiness.

"When you look at many of the things in Walter's collection—he has some very, *very* nice things—they tend to be the more flashy rather than the really subtle things," Sokolowski said. "Those were things that weren't fashionable at the moment, but time went with him. Walter's tastes were vindicated."

At the other extreme, Sokolowski, who has been the director of the Andy Warhol Museum in Pittsburgh since 1996, noted something Chrysler had in common with the iconic Pop artist. "He would go up and down the antique stores, and he would pick up crap. . . . The one I almost choked on when he was presenting it—it was so outrageous—was a Melamine chip-and-dip set." Sokolowski remembered that decorative arts curator Mark Clark was speechless. "And Walter sort of looked at him, and he said, 'Well, this is for the Walter Chrysler Educational Study Collection.' But then he would bring back wonderful things. Glass.

"I think if you want to understand the joy that was Walter and the humor and the brio, and you try to make him into this great scholarly collector, I'm sorry, that just wasn't the case. But he took the kind of brassy chances that [private collectors] would never take." Despite Chrysler's occasional lapses in judgment and taste, Sokolowski said, the museum contains "one of the better encyclopedic collections in the country."

During Steadman's tenure, acquisitions were for the most part focused on preparatory drawings for works already in the collection or works that were related to works in the collection. Thanks to Brooks Johnson's fund-raising efforts, the museum also began buying photographs. Steadman also recalled the purchase of contemporary glass. He and Chrysler carefully worked out the details of his periodic gifts to the museum—which paintings were especially needed, and when.

"Nothing went into the collection without my bringing it to the board, the Acquisitions Committee," Steadman said. "That was one of the places where professionalism was needed." In addition, Steadman and Stokes had to convince Chrysler that the museum's trustees had a responsibility to give, or raise, money—a big change from the way things were being done. Steadman also oversaw the registration and photographing of the museum's holdings—another important and time-consuming requirement for accreditation.

In November 1982, Jeff Harrison began working for the museum as a researcher. Up to that point there hadn't been much study of the collection. "Walter Chrysler was not someone interested in paperwork, paper trails," Harrison said. "In many cases research wasn't hard to do, because so many of the pictures he bought were certainly distinguished enough to retrieve the histories of them pretty easily, and we have a great library. It was pretty easy to reconstruct anything that had a British provenance right in-house," said Harrison.

One of the museum's top priorities was to mount exhibits that would attract the public. "One of the ones that was most fun was the Norfolk Tricentennial Show," said Steadman.

"That did bring in a lot of people. It showed the museum really cared about the city in which it was located. [But] I think the single most beautiful show we ever did while I was there was the one of the Tiffany lamps, all of which were in Walter's collection, most of which departed [after Walter's death]. But it was literally one of the most beautiful shows I've ever seen. And the public loved it."

Harrison credits Steadman with helping to tame the "Wild West" nature of the museum. "There was a hierarchy in place. There were standards in place," he said. "Walter had taken his hands off the wheel."

16

FAREWELL TO
A DEVOTED
PARTNER

In December 1981, at the age of sixty, Jean Outland Chrysler suffered a stroke. For her husband of thirty-seven years, the series of events that followed must have seemed a dreadful echo of those leading to his mother's death. Now Walter Chrysler stood to lose a devoted partner, a loyal champion, and a good friend.

Edythe Harrison, founder of the Virginia Opera Association and a close friend of the couple, happened to see Chrysler in New York shortly after he'd heard the news of his wife's hospitalization. "On one of the most tragic days I can remember," Harrison said, "I was waiting for one of my children to get off a plane. Walter came running through the airport and saw me there just by coincidence. He told me Jean had had a cerebral hemorrhage and he was going to Norfolk. I sat with him in shock, [and] I tried to comfort him. 'What are we going to do?' he said. 'How can we save Jean?' I felt, at some level, her determination would pull her out and she'd be back, standing at the opera, talking to every patron."[1] Jean did not recover, however; she died on January 26, 1982.

Family, friends, and members of the arts community eulogized the generous, fun-loving, tireless champion of culture in her hometown. Her legacy included her gifts of modern art collections to her alma mater, the College of William and Mary, as well as to the Chrysler; and her pride and joy, the outstanding Jean Outland Chrysler Art Reference Library, which she had nurtured from its infancy.

But if her feelings for the library were maternal, what she felt for the opera was a lover's passion. When the relatively new organization presented the world premiere of Thea Musgrave's *Mary, Queen of Scots,* Norfolk's Center Theater had been neglected for so long it was still in disrepair on the eve of the performance. "Jean and I were there with the painters," Harrison recalled. "She was painting! She was tacking down the carpet! There was no job too small for Jean if something had to be done. She would roll up her sleeves."

Catherine Jordan Wass, now the museum's deputy director, remembered how thrilled Jean was when Luciano Pavarotti came to town in 1981, not long before she died. The famous tenor performed at Chrysler Hall. Included in the price of the $100 ticket was an invitation to an after-performance reception. Wass recalled that Jean felt as though it were her party. "She had on a beautiful gown," Wass said. "I felt like she had one last chance to wear something really beautiful. And she seemed so happy. It was this last hurrah for her. Maybe she had a sense of Norfolk and this area coming into its own."[2]

"Jean was funny," said Edythe Harrison. "And she became friendly with every singer that came to the opera. She was at the epicenter of everything we did. And as plain as Jean was—there were no pretenses—she knew quality." Irene Roughton, the Chrysler's associate registrar, remembered Jean Chrysler as lively and optimistic. "She had no distinctions of class," she said. "Everybody was everybody."[3] "Walter

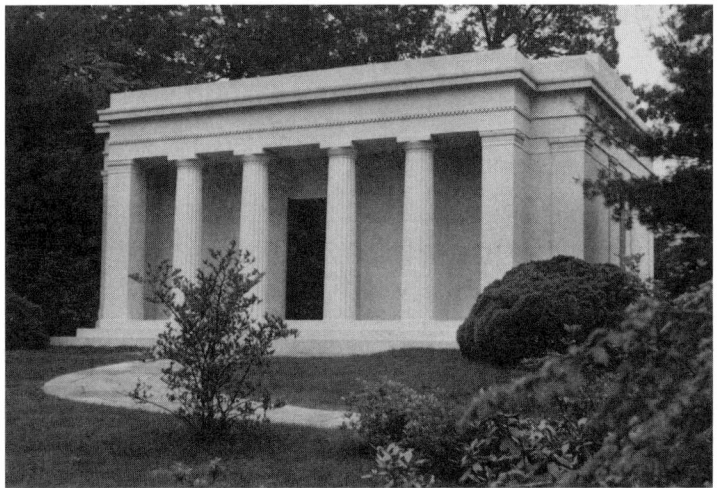

The Chrysler family mausoleum at Sleepy Hollow Cemetery in Tarrytown, New York. Walter and Jean Chrysler are both interred there. (Courtesy of the Chrysler Museum of Art, Norfolk, Va.)

was in shock when Jean died," her older sister, Louise Outland Smith, said. "She'd put up with him. He had lost his best friend."

A reporter who attended a gathering at the Chryslers' home two days after Jean's death heard those very words from her widower. Chrysler, he wrote, "loved her very much and said so Wednesday, wrapped as he was in the armor of shock that produces a strange kind of clarity in the remembering. . . . She was, he said, an independent woman, strong-willed and full of drive, who came into her own as a lover of not only art, but the quality of life that helps produce it. . . . Sitting in the parlor, his eyes welling with tears, Chrysler said, 'We were a team, Jean and I. I guess the most important thing was I could be a pal to Jean. And she could be a pal to me.' "[4]

Julie Dalton noted how much Chrysler had depended

on his wife. "I think Jean kept him on an even keel that he missed. She fed him, and she was there." After Jean's death, said Dalton, "Walter disintegrated, more or less."

In New York's Hudson River Valley, just outside Tarrytown, is the picturesque Sleepy Hollow Cemetery. It was named by the popular American author Washington Irving, who is buried there alongside Andrew Carnegie, William Rockefeller, and Samuel Gompers. It is also the site of the imposing Doric-columned mausoleum where members of the Chrysler family lie. Joining them there, on January 30, 1982, was Jean Outland Chrysler.

17

A DIAMOND JUBILEE

About six months after Jean Chrysler's death, an assistant was hired for glass curator Nancy Merrill. Gary Baker, who would eventually serve as glass curator himself, arrived with "no preconceived ideas about Walter," but he came to show him "the respect I would a loaded revolver. You never knew exactly where his mind was going. You never knew which buttons were the wrong ones."

Baker recalled a New York shopping trip with Chrysler and Merrill. "A pretty amazing experience," he said. "Walter took us to his favorite Tiffany dealer, Minna Rosenblatt. We went into that shop together, and we went to a place at the southern end of New York that mainly catered to the decorating trade. He wanted my immediate opinions on everything, whether I knew anything about it or not. We bought four objects that day.

"When we got back to his apartment, we had drinks around a card table. It was amazing to watch him. He wanted to unpack each of his purchases and look at them on the table. He beamed and said, 'Now let's gloat!' And I think, totally, he spent no more than a thousand dollars that day."

Chrysler's apartment was furnished primarily in Art Deco–style furniture. Baker remembered Nancy Merrill showing him a bronze head of Walter as a young man. A few years later, after Chrysler died, Baker was up in New York at Sotheby's and discovered the bronze head in an arcade sale. "I looked in the back of it, and there were paint spots, and I remembered there had been a lot of paint spilled by his house painters on his Art Deco furniture. Then I saw this wacky Provincetown numbering system he had used. It said 'SC' for sculpture. I checked it, and it said 'Estate of Walter Chrysler.'"

Baker had some trouble convincing then-director Robert Frankel to go after the head. Baker said, "I talked him into putting up some money, and I had a good friend, a glass expert, who lived in New York a few blocks from Sotheby's. He went and represented us so no one would know. He barely got that head. It's now out in the front lobby."

Five hundred people crowded onto the lawn outside the museum in May 1984 to help celebrate Walter Chrysler's seventy-fifth birthday. Greetings arrived from Virginia's governor and state senators, and the guests ate a cake baked in the shape of the museum as it would look after a planned $8-million expansion. The addition would provide galleries for a large number of holdings that had been hidden in storage since Chrysler's arrival.

Chrysler marked his diamond jubilee with extravagant praise for his adopted city, calling Norfolk "the gateway to the South" and adding, "I'm sure if we had a Civil War today, Norfolk would be the capital of the South."[1] He bolstered his words with the donation of ten important paintings that had previously been on loan, estimated to be worth some $10 million. The works covered four centuries and several countries, including a mid-fifteenth-century portrait by

Domenico Veneziano; Carlo Crivelli's *St. Anthony of Padua;* Filippino Lippi's *Madonna and Child Enthroned;* a small portrait by Velázquez, a Delacroix, a Winslow Homer, an Edward Hopper, and a Jackson Pollock.[2] David Steadman called the paintings "a dream gift," adding, "Not since Mr. Chrysler's original gift of a major portion of his collection in 1971 has the museum received such a splendid and important group of paintings."[3]

The expansion, for which the Washington, D.C., architecture firm of Hartman-Cox was hired, would enlarge the museum by 43,000 square feet and renovate about a third of the existing 94,000 square feet. The main entrance would receive a new façade after its move from Olney Road to its original placement, opening onto the picturesque Hague inlet. The entire structure would be made more symmetrical by adding a second tower and a north wing.[4]

Chrysler was about to resign as chairman and member of the board of trustees. "I look forward to the chance to sit back and watch what it becomes," he said. "Everything is being left in the best hands and is going in the best direction possible. I think I will enjoy being in Norfolk more. I'll be more relaxed with no particular burdens to face, hopefully, and more fully enjoy the friends Jean and I have made.'"[5]

Early in 1985, Roger D. Clisby was named deputy director and chief curator of the Chrysler, replacing Tom Sokolowski. Clisby, who died in 1994, came to Norfolk from the Crocker Art Museum in Sacramento, California, where he had been chief curator for fourteen years. His duties included administration and budget as well as the preservation, interpretation, and exhibition of the museum's art. This was meant to give David Steadman more time to focus on the upcoming building project and do more long-range planning.[6]

Two years later, the museum acquired a stellar addition to

its collection. In February 1987, after a year and a half of negotiations, the Chrysler obtained seventy neoclassical sculptures from the James H. Ricau collection. A retired businessman, Ricau donated some of the works, and the museum purchased the rest. Included in the group were thirty-nine full-figure sculptures, twenty-eight busts, and three reliefs, most carved from white Carrara marble. Steadman told a reporter that the new additions gave the museum "one of the finest 19th-century American sculpture collections in this country." He added that Ricau chose the Chrysler because it had the space to keep all the works together, while other interested museums could not.[7]

Another important collection arrived in 1988. Edwin Pearlman, a Norfolk eye surgeon, donated one hundred Mayan ceramic plates, vessels, and sculptures, predominantly from the Classic period (AD 300–900).[8]

Brooks Johnson became the museum's full-time photography curator in 1985. He noted that this department was the only major one at the museum developed without Chrysler's involvement. "When we did our first show in the photography gallery, we borrowed work from a private collection," Johnson said. "People who were our major photography benefactors made it possible. We received exactly fifty photographs from Mr. Chrysler. Those were mostly portraits of artists in his collection. There were about six Edward Steichen photographs, because he knew him."

Johnson remembered a spat he had with Chrysler over the introductory label in the new photography gallery that opened in 1988. Chrysler was miffed because the label didn't mention the Chrysler Museum. Johnson explained that, since the photographs were not owned by the museum, there was no need to include the Chrysler name on the label.

"It was later that I realized what that was really about,"

Johnson said. "That photography was growing inside of his museum, and he wasn't a part of it. In a way he probably viewed it as a cancer. There is a good ending to the story, though," Johnson said. "And that is, when he died, he did this weird thing where he divvied up percentages for endowments. He left an endowment for photography. It was the smallest of all of them, but at least he left something. And that was really meaningful to me because it meant that he had accepted photography and wanted to be part of it and wanted it to continue in his museum."

18

Heir to a Fortune

In the summer of 1988, Walter Chrysler was seventy-nine and in the final stages of prostate cancer. His health had been declining for some time and photos taken during that period show it: Although he still had a full head of pure white hair, his formerly round, fleshy face now seemed fragile and birdlike, his cheeks were concave, and the once-portly figure appeared to have withered.

Chrysler had never talked about death and apparently didn't like to think about dying. Now, however, he confided in those close to him. "I was one of those people who thought that Walter was going to live forever," said Linda Kaufman, who had been an active museum trustee for many years. "I remember one day, he said to me, 'Linda, I've got cancer,' just like you'd say, 'It might rain tomorrow.' I was just struck because he and the museum were such a part of my life."

Ron Kuchta was the director of the Everson Museum in Syracuse, New York, when David Steadman called him. "He didn't think Walter would live much longer," Kuchta said. "If I wanted to see him again, I should come down to Norfolk. So I did. He was in bed at home. He looked a little flushed but seemed to have his wits about him. He said to me, 'Ron, you know I have cancer and I'm going to die.' He was very matter-of-fact about it. He said, 'I'm not leaving you anything in my will. But I consider that I gave you your career.'"

Arthur Diamonstein was part of Chrysler's Norfolk inner circle who, with Lane Stokes and Phil Trapani, realized it was essential for a new will to be drawn up to ensure that the museum would receive all the pieces still officially "on loan." "Close to his death, I spent time with him," Diamonstein said. "Walter trusted very few people. He didn't want to talk to any lawyers. He hated lawyers. He only wanted to talk to Phil Trapani, our city attorney at the time. And he trusted me and Lane Stokes. I worked with him in the afternoons and the evenings to help him with his will."[1]

But Trapani had troubles of his own. His wife had been in an auto accident, and he was in the hospital with a burst appendix and peritonitis. "A whole series of things delayed [the signing of the will]," said Diamonstein. "I begged Walter to get someone else, another lawyer, to do it. He wouldn't have it. So we sat up there in his house and talked about the will and what he wanted to do with it and [that] he wanted to leave this here and that there."

Former Norfolk city manager James Oliver said he was not surprised by Chrysler's stubborn insistence on dealing only with Phil Trapani. "On a personal level, Phil reached out to Walter without ever compromising the role he was playing," Oliver said. "But, on the other hand, [he was not] so cautious that he kept a distance. That has to have been very important."[2]

According to Diamonstein, Jack Tanzer and Chrysler had had a falling out a few months before Chrysler died. When it was apparent that time was short, Renée Diamonstein called Tanzer and said, "You better get down here. Things are not good." The Diamonsteins picked Tanzer up at the airport that Saturday morning, and he spent five or six hours with Chrysler. "They got back together again," Diamonstein said. "We took him back to the airport. Next thing we heard, Walter had died.

"We had arranged for him to sign the new will on a Monday morning at 10 o'clock," Diamonstein said. "He died Saturday night before that. But he truly wanted to sign the new will. There are those who say he didn't. But I know he did." Tanzer concurred. "I'm *amazed* that Walter let those works go elsewhere," he said. "I can't believe that. It was his life's work."[3]

Ron Kuchta is also convinced that Chrysler intended to sign the new will. "I think he was holding out. I don't think he thought he would die then. In fact, he pretty much told me that on the phone. His whole purpose, his whole objective, was to preserve the Chrysler name. He said, 'The Chrysler collection will outlive by far the Chrysler Corporation,' So his nephew, Jack, really fell into it," Kuchta said. "I don't think he'd seen him nor had much to do with him, ever. That was unfortunate."

Jeff Harrison said, "There were fifteen to twenty works I would have killed to keep. But 95 percent of what was great was already locked down, so what was left—I mean the great Géricault, that's gone; early-nineteenth-century things—that's where we were hardest hit. When he died, I think we lost about fourteen Tiffany lamps that were on loan, some of them very rare," Gary Baker said. "He was buying stuff until he got too sick to go out of his house. Once he owned something for a while, it was like baseball cards, he would trade and cash in. Having stuff on loan gave him currency as his taste shifted.

"In 1987, he bought some major Tiffany pieces—blown glass, lava pieces—that he had on loan to us. Those left. Generally speaking, except for the lamps, most of the glass had been given. He had given a lot, but for tax purposes he couldn't give everything at once. He intended to do it. At the same time, I'm sure he wanted to wrest concessions out of the museum administration, the things he wanted done with the building as it was being redone," Baker said.

"You could never pin him down, you could never get him into focus, and it just makes sense that he would go out with that kind of chaotic flourish," noted Harrison. "It was a poker game from start to finish. The last couple of cards weren't nice. But the game was ours."

Typically, opinions of Chrysler's intentions varied widely. Tommy Willcox, who was president of the museum board when Chrysler died, pointed out that he "never committed his whole collection at any time. I don't think anyone should fault Walter for wanting to give to his family."[4] Louise Outland Smith was more adamant. "At the time, I said anybody would know that he isn't going to leave a nickel to anybody who isn't a Chrysler. I knew that about him. I know what he meant to do. He meant to leave it all to Jack."

Jack Forker Chrysler Jr. has his own theory as to why he became his uncle's beneficiary, recalling a melancholy final conversation. "I was in the hospital with Walter a few days before he died," he said. "I really liked Walter. I got along with him better than most people in the family [did]. I think it was because he really loved my dad."[5]

Jack Chrysler remembers offering to take his uncle over to the museum in a wheelchair so he could see the nearly completed renovation. Chrysler refused to go. "It was just too tough for him, too emotional. He was very proud of the museum, but I got the impression that, especially with the new wing, he felt he had lost control, that people were usurping him and his opinion. And that's why he didn't want to see it.

"When I was at the hospital, he said to me, 'I'm going to give all the money to the museum,'" Jack Chrysler recalled. "And I said, 'Well, it's your money, Walter. You should do whatever you want with it.' And he kind of cried and smiled, and I was looking out the window, and I had tears in my eyes because he was really in bad shape."

Jack Chrysler interpreted that exchange as his uncle's way of gauging his reaction to the news—a sort of test. "You see, Walter was that kind of guy," he said. "He was pretty sly, very bright. He could be real tricky. I don't know whether he had two wills or whether that existed at all. Then, as it turned out, he had a will with Kelley Drye, which has been the family law firm for years and years in New York. That was the last signed will. And Harvey Zimand from Kelley Drye called me up and said, 'Jack, you're a big part of this will.' Up until that day, I didn't know I was going to receive anything from him.

"I was stunned. But my sister and I didn't get anything at all from our own mother. I think Walter knew that, and because of his relationship with my dad, I think he felt that I was the one that he was going to leave things with."

Ann Vernon, the museum's education director, said, "It was very interesting, because I knew the Chryslers personally. And because I knew Nina [Newby Ireland, a friend and employee of the Chryslers], I knew that Walter had always juggled his will. To an outsider, he'd kind of play cat and mouse with his will. But to an insider, you'd say how smart he was because of the income tax. If he gives X number of millions of dollars of paintings each year, he can avoid the horrible income taxes, and so forth."

On Tuesday, September 20, a thirty-minute memorial was held at the Church of the Good Shepherd in Norfolk and attended by about three hundred people. Burial took place the next day in the Chrysler mausoleum in Tarrytown. Another memorial was held a day later in Manhattan, at St. Bartholomew's church, the site of Walter Chrysler's first wedding. Jack Chrysler described the funeral as "sad, mostly family, pretty private."

19

THE AUCTION BLOCK

On October 12, 1988, David Steadman announced Walter Chrysler's bequest to the museum. In accordance with his only legal will, seventeen American and European paintings, a $1.6-million endowment, and 76 percent of an estimated $5-million family trust fund went to the Chrysler Museum.

Steadman said he was surprised to learn that most of Chrysler's artwork that was still on loan to the museum, 751 separate objects, were bequeathed to his nephew, "the only male of his generation bearing the Chrysler name." The inheritance included 120 paintings as well as several hundred objects from the eight-thousand-piece glass collection.[1]

"When that happened, let me tell you, the Chrysler staff, who had been here and loved Walter and loved the collection, was just devastated," said Ann Vernon. "We suddenly saw the collection dispersed." That said, the majority of the works going to Jack Chrysler were in storage. Only about thirty of them had been on display at the museum. David Steadman noted that the Chrysler's most important works, such as Bernini's *Bust of the Savior* and Gauguin's

Loss of Virginity, would remain with the museum. He said there would be no problem filling the newly expanded galleries due to open in February.

Jack Chrysler flew in from California to attend a ceremony at the museum in his uncle's honor. When the ceremony was over, said Vernon, "Tommy Willcox realized that Jack was there, and we all knew that Jack was inheriting from the old will. Tommy said, 'Ann, why don't you take Jack around through the Ancient Worlds,' because he knew that we didn't have an Ancient Worlds curator. I took him around and showed him all these little things that I thought, 'This is critical, this is critical, this is critical.'

"The main thing he said was that we could keep the wooden *Striding Attendant,* Vernon said, "and that was the piece that I then saw going on the back of a truck! And I ran to [museum administrator] Roger Clisby and said, 'But Jack Chrysler said we could keep this!' And Roger went down and got it loaded off. So it came back.

"There were other pieces that I pointed out to Jack. He basically gave a green light to just about everything in the Ancient Worlds collection. I can't really remember anything that he said we couldn't keep," Vernon said. "He understood that, at that point, all sixth-graders came through Ancient Worlds, and he was very generous about that."

Asked why Chrysler didn't leave anything to another nephew and four nieces, Raymond French, who was married to one of the nieces and coexecutor of the will, replied, "He was just that way." Steadman interpreted it as "very Old World." Focusing on the positive, he acknowledged Chrysler's "princely gifts" to the museum, which he said were worth about $100 million.

The trust fund had been established by Walter Chrysler Sr. and had been his son's main source of income during his life. Twelve percent of the fund was slated for the Virginia

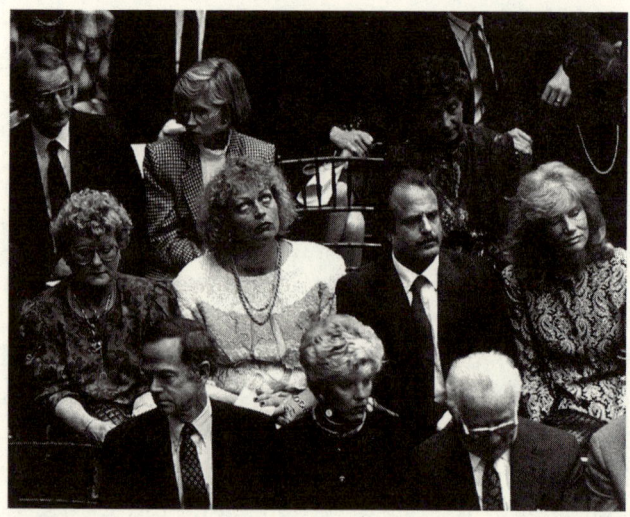

Jack Chrysler Jr., seated in the middle row, attends the Sotheby's auction in 1989, where some of the art he inherited from his uncle Walter set sales records. Walter died two days before he was scheduled to sign a codicil to his will, in which he would have left everything to the Chrysler Museum. (Courtesy of the *Norfolk Virginian-Pilot*.)

Opera Association, to be used specifically for hiring the finest singers for its productions. The museum's endowment was divided into percentages earmarked for various uses—mostly for purchasing art—but was contingent on the raising of matching funds.

Officials from Sotheby's New York auction house announced that the 751-piece art collection inherited by Jack Forker Chrysler Jr. would be sold in June 1989. Part of the proceeds would go toward paying estate taxes that, at that time, equaled half the estate's value.[2]

On May 31, 1989, 128 of Walter's paintings were offered in what Sotheby's called "the most important collection of Old

Masters to come up for auction in 28 years."[3] The Chrysler Museum's leadership said it had no intention of bidding on any of the auctioned works themselves. Some one thousand people crowded into Sotheby's for the auction, including museum directors, dealers, and collectors. Paintings sold at an average of one per minute. Only 4 percent of the pictures didn't sell because their reserve prices weren't met.[4] The auction brought in more than $18.5 million, exceeding the auction house's highest estimate.

"Some dealers were rather supercilious about Chrysler's buying in the post-War period," observed the *Financial Times* (of London), "considering that his taste lacked refinement. But as record followed record the auction began to resemble an Impressionist sale. . . . The demand at the sale was reassuringly widespread, with dealers from many countries competing against collectors."[5]

Another auction, for 230 Art Deco and Art Nouveau objects, including many Tiffany lamps, took place on June 16. Once again, almost everything sold, and estimates were topped; the auction brought in $2.38 million.[6] Minna Rosenblatt was there and was able to leave with some of the pieces that, years earlier, she had sold to Walter Chrysler.

20

"A Priceless Blessing"

Newly enlarged and renovated, the Chrysler Museum officially opened to the public on February 26, 1989, after several days of invitation-only previews and parties. That Sunday afternoon anyone could enter the building that for the past few years had been a construction site and see what $13.5 million dollars had bought and what the 50 percent additional space held.

Under several levels of European-style red-tiled roofs, a handsome colonnade led to glass entry doors. A few marble steps took visitors up to the splendid expanse of Huber Court, a dramatic atrium and the architectural centerpiece of the Chrysler. Flooded with natural light, the court's wood-beamed ceiling was fashioned into a peaked roof of glass. From the center of the checkerboard slate floor, rooms fanned out in three directions.

To the left were the gift shop and two galleries for changing exhibits, one of which contained the Ricau sculpture collection, on view for the first time against deep green walls. To the right was the new Institute of Glass, with ten redesigned galleries featuring Walter Chrysler's eight-thousand-piece glass collection. Chronologically arranged, the collection included works from ancient Rome through modern jewel-colored lamps by Tiffany.

Ahead, through an arched doorway, could be found exhibits containing works from the ancient worlds: Greco-Roman, Indian, Oriental, Egyptian, pre-Colombian. The right rear of the building contained the restaurant, the theater, and the Jean Outland Chrysler Library, which had at last settled into its proper home within the museum's walls.

Leading upstairs from Huber Court, an elegant double staircase climbed to the second-floor galleries. From the balcony, visitors could see enticing samples of what the rooms encircling the atrium held, including decorative art and paintings and sculptures arranged by time period, with works dating from the Middle Ages to the modern era. Finally, beside the Alice and Sol B. Frank Photography Galleries, a large space was earmarked for photography and conservation studios.

Journalists from as far away as France and Germany, as well as writers from tony magazines like *Connoisseur* and *Town and Country,* came to record the grand reopening of the Chrysler. Among the extravagant reviews was one from *Architectural Record:* "The museum today is a stately assemblage of Florentine Renaissance-inspired elements around a covered central courtyard." Instead of a "hodgepodge of additions," the Chrysler "is a museum that reads as a unified building."[1] Paul Goldberger of the *New York Times* called the Chrysler "a building of considerable strength and self-assurance."[2]

Two days after the unveiling, David Steadman announced he would be leaving to direct the Toledo (Ohio) Museum of Art. About three months after Steadman's departure, a new director was hired. Robert Frankel came to Norfolk from the Center for Fine Arts in Miami. It was an enormous change for the forty-six-year-old Cincinnati native. The differences between the Miami arts center and the Chrysler were dramatic. The Chrysler's building was almost five times bigger; it contained a major permanent collection (the Miami arts center depended on temporary shows); and its budget topped Miami's by nearly $1 million.[3]

Frankel's mission, as he saw it, was to excite local interest in the museum with a string of traveling exhibits. During his six-year tenure, he accomplished that goal. Membership increased by a third, and although a budget reduction occurred, that was blamed on city, state, and national cutbacks. Frankel left the Chrysler in 1995 to take a position as executive director of the Santa Barbara Museum of Art. Only one year later, the Chrysler was in serious trouble. A $500,000 deficit translated into staff layoffs, the cancellation of scheduled exhibits, and the institution of its first mandatory admission charge. Worse yet, the museum had drained $1 million from a rainy-day fund willed to it by the museum's late benefactor. To deplete it, said board president Roy Martin, was tantamount to "selling off the family jewels." Nevertheless, Martin insisted that a strategic plan was in the works.[4]

In January 1997, after a fourteen-month search and about one hundred applicants, the Chrysler announced the hiring of a new director, the sixth since Walter Chrysler's arrival in 1971. William J. Hennessey had been director of the University of Michigan Museum of Art in Ann Arbor and, before that, the University of Kentucky Art Museum in Lexington and the Vassar College Art Gallery in Poughkeepsie, New York.

The new director saw one of his key challenges to be the reshaping of the Chrysler's mission to make the museum a more integral part of community life. He talked about balancing programming ambitions with available resources and continuing the process of raising professional standards, which began when Walter Chrysler relinquished control. Even allowing for significantly increased trustee giving, Hennessey noted, the Chrysler now had a very small budget for the size of its collection—thirty thousand objects—and for the physical size of its building and the range of its programs. That, combined with a community that was neither large nor wealthy, made the challenge of offering top-quality programs even more daunting.[5]

Hennessey identified two possible ways of meeting that challenge. One was to raise more money. Realistically, however, he saw the operating budget growing only modestly; the other approach was to work creatively, to focus exhibitions and programs on what the Chrysler could do that nobody else could. Hennessey explained that the museum would have to continue to earn its place at the heart of the educational, social, and economic life of the community. "We need to offer people a chance to learn about themselves and their world, to engage seriously with ideas and to enjoy themselves with their friends and family," he said.

Hennessey said he was committed to ensuring that the museum's permanent collection continued to grow, but he also stressed the importance of traveling shows as a way to keep the museum alive and attract new visitors. Those shows cost a great deal of money, he said, which begs the question, "If one didn't invest in those traveling exhibitions, what could one do with the art that's already here, to present it in more exciting and fresh ways?" One answer to that question has been provided—by none other than Walter P. Chrysler Jr.

In the fall of 2005, an exciting exhibit was held that featured work from museum storage: Behind the Seen: The Chrysler's Hidden Museum. "It's only a fraction of what we have in storage," Jeff Harrison said. "One could do a series of these shows." He felt the show gave viewers "a sense of the real riches we have here and, hopefully, they'll want us to show it all—and we'll say we need more space. Give more money so we can build something." Even veteran volunteers, said Harrison, got to see things they'd never seen before.

Ninety-five percent of the exhibit, in excess of two hundred pieces of painting, sculpture, prints, drawings, and books, came from Walter Chrysler's original gift to the museum.

21

LEGACY

Walter Chrysler often said he didn't care in the least how he would be remembered after his death. In fact, he told a reporter, he wouldn't want an obituary because there were things in his life he didn't want people to know. But the passage of time and the perspective it brings have been mostly kind to the man who often seemed a target for snipers, both in the press and from within the museum he endowed.

"I think that nobody in the arts will ever compare with what Walter Chrysler did for Hampton Roads," said Joshua P. Darden Jr., a Norfolk businessman, philanthropist, and former Chrysler Museum trustee. "It was a fabulous gift we got, particularly for a community that's not wealthy, as we're not. When you think of the Norfolk Society of the Arts and the little museum we had down there compared with what it is now, it's unbelievable. People are really stunned when they see the breadth of the collection."[1]

In a 1991 article, the *New York Times* called Walter Chrysler "the most underrated American art collector of the past 50 years and more." Chrysler's method of choosing art was described as being "completely in line with today's taste. . . . Walter Chrysler went his own way at his own pace. A strong and uncompromising nature permeates every room of the Chrysler Museum, and that nature carries us along by the sheer force of its commitment."[2]

Even Hilton Kramer, the art critic whose brief stay in Norfolk was spoiled by Chrysler's practical joke, grudgingly acknowledged his legacy. Kramer wrote that Chrysler, "through the odd course of his peregrinations in the art world, managed to acquire, despite the fakes, the overly optimistic attributions, and the unwise sale of objects sometimes superior to those he retained, a collection of undoubted museum quality. Which is to say that he managed to convert a sometimes uncontrollable obsession into an aesthetic enterprise of public importance. The result is the small-scale but utterly delightful Chrysler Museum in Norfolk, Virginia." Kramer sprinkled a final dash of vengeance into the mix, adding "the art in the collection told another story—the story of a collector who, however eccentric his taste could be at times and however atrocious his manners might be at all times, knew what he was doing most of the time when it came to buying art." Kramer concluded that Chrysler's story had a happy ending, in which "an expanded and resplendent Chrysler Museum now stands as an admirable monument to the curious character—one of the last of the old-style aesthete-connoisseurs—who made it possible."[3]

Among the speakers at the 1989 museum dedication ceremony was Evan H. Turner, director of the Cleveland Museum of Art, and a consultant to the Chrysler during its expansion and renovation. "As his mercurial career made amply clear, Walter Chrysler was a true eccentric," Turner said, and praised Chrysler's "single-minded vision" and "fervor to persuade others to follow."[4]

His vision is, naturally, most obvious in the city that became

Walter Chrysler's second home. Upon his death, a *Virginian-Pilot* editorial declared, "His collection revitalized the arts across Hampton Roads" and bestowed upon the area "a priceless blessing."[5] Soon afterward, Tom Styron, the former Chrysler curator of American and contemporary art, told the *Pilot:* "He could have built a monument to his own taste. Instead, he created the community's most valuable resource."[6] True, said Jack Chrysler. "When you reflect back, you'll see that out of the whole family, with the exception of my grandfather, Walter's made the biggest contribution of anybody."

Walter P. Chrysler Jr. did not live long enough to witness the opening of the newly glorious Chrysler Museum, but he still managed to have his say. At the dedication ceremony, David Steadman read these words written a year earlier by the museum's eponym and chief benefactor:

"There is a realm of spirit which lies low across the environment, apart from and beyond the stiff, unbending structures of ideology. It is the realm of the inquiring spirit, of minds that refuse to stop learning, of intellectuals who are willing to seek out other cultures, to share in the achievements of those cultures and to take us out into new fields. . . . The most efficient knowledge has been, and is, the cultural communication that has survived from one generation to another, from one civilization to the next, and from one city to another.

"Human enterprise conjured out of the earth's new metropolises—Venice, Florence, Paris, London, New York—and now Norfolk, that with the affirmation of this great Beaux Arts edifice refuses to overlook the contributions of the past. That is what I have found here in Norfolk—that realm of the inquiring spirit, of the minds that refuse to stop learning, of intellectuals who are and have been willing to seek out other cultures to share in their accomplishments."[7]

AFTERWORD

More than three decades after Walter Chrysler bestowed his gift of art to Norfolk, it is still called "unmatched in modern Virginia history," and its value is "estimated at between $750 million and $1 billion."

In the fall of 2002, to honor the thirtieth anniversary of that gift, the Chrysler Museum's board unveiled a $30-million capital campaign.[1] When that amount was raised, the goal was elevated to $40 million. At the time of this writing, Bill Hennessey said that more than $34 million had been pledged, resulting in the renovation of the museum's George and Linda Kaufman Theatre, the creation of the Norfolk History Museum, the building of the Norfolk Foundation Center for Art Education, and the doubling of the museum's endowment for operations.[2]

NOTES

1. ROSEBUD

1. Jack Tanzer, telephone interview by the author, January 12, 2005.

2. Earl Swift and Teresa Annas, "Museum Missed Chrysler Treasure by Hours: Benefactor Died Less Than 2 Days before Meeting to Sign New Will, *Norfolk Virginian-Pilot and Ledger-Star,* April 9, 1989. All subsequent citations of the *Virginian-Pilot* refer to the *Norfolk Virginian-Pilot.* Citations of the *Ledger-Star* refer to the afternoon edition of the *Norfolk Virginian-Pilot.*

2. THE NORFOLK MUSEUM OF ARTS AND SCIENCES

1. Jo Ann Mervis Hofheimer, *Annie Wood: A Portrait: The Life and Times of the Founder of the Irene Leache Memorial* (Norfolk: Irene Leache Memorial, 1976), 97.

2. Joe Fahy, "More Than Space Is at Stake in Chrysler Expansion," *Virginian-Pilot and Ledger-Star,* August 4, 1985.

3. Hofheimer, *Annie Wood,* 109.

4. "Norfolk Museum of Arts and Sciences Is Reality: Opens with Exhibit Today," *Virginian-Pilot,* March 5, 1933.

5. Hofheimer, *Annie Wood,* 111–12.

6. Robert H. Mason, "In Museumland," typescript.

7. "A Florentine Palace and a Princely Gift," editorial, *Virginian-Pilot,* September 23, 1960.

8. Matthew Werth, interview by the author, May 27, 2004. Unless otherwise noted, all subsequent quotations by Matthew Werth are from this interview.

9. William L. Tazewell, "A Growing Museum in Transition," *Virginian-Pilot,* September 1, 1963.

10. "Membership of Museum Integrated," *Norfolk Ledger-Dispatch,* May 12, 1964.

11. F. D. Cossitt, "Norfolk Museum at the Crossroads," *Virginian-Pilot,* April 12, 1972.

12. George Holbert Tucker, "Museum Gets Italian Art: Chrysler Collection to Launch New Wing," *Virginian-Pilot,* May 21, 1967.

13. "Museum Funds Held Back," *Virginian-Pilot,* July 24, 1968.

14. "Chrysler Appointed to Museum Board." *Virginian-Pilot,* January 22, 1969.

3. The Auto Baron's Son

1. Walter P. Chrysler, in collaboration with Boyden Sparks, *Life of an American Workman* (New York: Saturday Evening Post/Curtis, 1937), 13.

2. Muriel B. Christison, "The Chrysler Story," typescript, ca. 1946, Standing files, Jean Outland Chrysler Art Library.

3. Chrysler, *Life of an American Workman,* 112.

4. Ibid, 164.

5. Vincent Curcio, *Chrysler: The Life and Times of an Automotive Genius* (New York: Oxford University Press, 2000), 307.

6. Christison, "The Chrysler Story."

7. Bob Lipper, "A Search for Self, a Stab at Immortality," *Virginian-Pilot,* July 3, 1977.

8. This was the way Chrysler usually told it. But in another version, he bought the painting with money he'd saved from his allowance.

9. Lipper, "A Search for Self."

10. Curcio, *Life and Times of an Automotive Genius,* 454.

11. Lipper, "A Search for Self."

12. Chrysler, *Life of an American Workman,* 208.

13. "Chrysler Building," New York History, www.newyorkhistory
.info/42nd-Street/chryslerbuilding.html.

14. Chrysler, *Life of an American Workman*, 199.

15. Thomas Connors, "Saga of a Compulsive Collector." *M*
magazine, June 1989, 4–6.

16. John Russell, "Time Rescues a Collector's Reputation," *New
York Times*, August 11, 1991.

17. Connors, "Saga of a Compulsive Collector."

18. "Temperature Corp," *Time*, July 23, 1934.

19. Curcio, *Life and Times of an Automotive Genius*, 623.

20. Margaret Scolari Barr, "Our Campaigns," *New Criterion*
(Summer 1987): 47.

21. Chris Hemphill. "Walter P. Chrysler Jr.: How I Made $1.6
Million from a $450 Picasso," *Interview*, June 1978, 38.

22. Linda McGreevy, "Happy Birthday Walter Chrysler!" *Port
Folio*, 2, no. 4 (May 22–28, 1984): 5–6.

23. "Society's 'Most-Sought Girl' Won by Heir," *Ironwood (Michigan) Daily Globe*, February 7, 1938.

24. Dr. Marguerite Nichols, interview by the author, June 10,
2004. Unless otherwise noted, all subsequent quotations by Dr.
Nichols are from this interview.

25. "Marguerite Sykes Has Church Bridal," *New York Times*,
April 30, 1938.

26. Curcio, *Life and Times of an Automotive Genius*, 646.

27. "Marguerite Chrysler Awarded Reno Decree," *Reno Evening
Gazette*, December 5, 1939.

28. Curcio, *Life and Times of an Automotive Genius*, 658.

29. "Walter P. Chrysler," editorial, *New York Times*, August 20,
1940.

30. "Chrysler Art on View," *New York Times*, February 2, 1941.

31. Isabelle Ziegler, "First Formal Exhibition of Tradition Shat-
ters Nerves of Audience: Art or Spinach?" *Richmond News Leader*,
January 17, 1941.

4. Walter and Jean

1. South Norfolk became a city in 1950 and, in 1963, was an-
nexed by the City of Chesapeake.

2. Louise Outland Smith, interview by the author, April 25, 2004. Unless otherwise noted, all subsequent quotations by Louise Outland Smith are from this interview.

3. Nancy Outland Chandler, interview by the author, February 19, 2004. Unless otherwise noted, all subsequent quotations by Nancy Outland Chandler are from this interview.

4. William Ruehlmann, "Man Behind the Museum," *Virginian-Pilot and Ledger-Star,* October 19, 1980.

5. Maureen Taylor, "Woman Behind the Man: Being Mrs. Chrysler Is 'Fun,'" *Ledger-Star,* November 29, 1967.

6. When details were requested under the Freedom of Information Act from the National Personnel Records Center, Military Personnel Records, St. Louis, Mo., the military refused to release the circumstances of Chrysler's "character discharge" from the navy to anyone but immediate family.

7. Curcio, *Life and Times of an Automotive Genius,* 659.

8. R. L. Blazevig, letter to the author, December 22, 2004.

9. Lipper, "A Search for Self."

10. "Miss Jean Outland Bride of Walter P. Chrysler Jr., at Freemason Street Church," *Virginian-Pilot,* January 14, 1945.

11. Grover Outland, interview by the author, February 25, 2004. Unless otherwise noted, all subsequent quotations by Grover Outland are from this interview.

12. Christison, "The Chrysler Story," 10.

13. Omeda Brockett, "Chrysler Art Collections Enjoyed by Many: Mrs. Chrysler Visits Parents in Norfolk," *Virginian-Pilot and Portsmouth Star,* April 8, 1956.

14. "Theatre Arts Spotlights: Walter P. Chrysler Jr.," *Theatre Arts,* September 1952, 21.

15. Ibid.

16. William J. Gill, "The Collector's Puzzling Path," *Life,* November 2, 1962, 100.

17. Lipper, "A Search for Self."

18. Curcio, *Life and Times of an Automotive Genius,* 659.

19. Ibid., 656–57.

20. Lipper, "A Search for Self."

21. Jefferson C. Harrison, interview by the author, February 13,

2004. Unless otherwise noted, all subsequent quotations by Jefferson Harrison are from this interview.

5. PROVINCETOWN

1. Peter Manso, *Ptown: Art, Sex, and Money on the Outer Cape* (New York: Scribner, 2002), 65.

2. Mary Ellen Butler, "Patron of the Past: Chrysler Brought Glamour and Great Masters, Then Departed Abruptly," *Provincetown Banner,* July 1, 1999.

3. Maureen Taylor, "Woman Behind the Man."

4. Minna Rosenblatt, interview by the author, February 29, 2004. Unless otherwise noted, all subsequent quotations by Minna Rosenblatt are from this interview.

5. Christopher Busa, interview by the author, July 20, 2004. Unless otherwise noted, all subsequent quotations by Christopher Busa are from this interview.

6. Ronald A. Kuchta, telephone interview by the author, April 16, 2004. Unless otherwise noted, all subsequent quotations by Ronald Kuchta are from this interview.

7. Nancy Merrill, interview by the author, January 3, 2004. Unless otherwise noted, all subsequent quotations by Nancy Merrill are from this interview.

8. Jack Tanzer, interview by the author, March 1, 2004.

9. Robert Kashey, telephone interview by the author, January 12, 2005. Unless otherwise noted, all subsequent quotations by Robert Kashey are from this interview.

6. THE COLLECTOR

1. "Forum: What Motivates a Person to Be a Collector of Art?" *American Artist,* November 1980, 12, 92.

2. David Steadman, telephone interview by the author, March 31, 2004. Unless otherwise noted, all subsequent quotations by David Steadman are from this interview.

3. Gary Baker, interview by the author, January 28, 2004. Unless otherwise noted, all subsequent quotations by Gary Baker are from this interview.

4. Mark Clark, interview by the author, February 7, 2004. Unless otherwise noted, all subsequent quotations by Mark Clark are from this interview.

5. Tom Sokolowski, interview by the author, March 19, 2004. Unless otherwise noted, all subsequent quotations by Tom Sokolowski are from this interview.

6. Ruehlmann, "Man Behind the Museum."

7. Tony Cacalano, telephone interview with the author, October 5, 2004. Unless otherwise noted, all subsequent quotations by Tony Cacalano are from this interview.

7. THE CONTROVERSIAL CENTURY

1. Connors, "Saga of a Compulsive Collector."

2. "Scent of Scandal," *Time*, October 26, 1962, 70.

3. "Fakes and Forgeries," Art Dealers Association Web site, www .artdealers.org/.

4. "Scent of Scandal."

5. "The Chrysler Affair," *Newsweek*, November 26, 1962.

6. "Scent of Scandal."

7. William J. Gill, "Strange Story of Walter Chrysler Jr. and the Great Art Scandal," *Life*, November 2, 1962, 93.

8. "Fakes and Forgeries."

9. Gill, "Collector's Puzzling Path."

10. Thomas Hoving, *False Impressions: The Hunt for Big-Time Art Fakes* (New York: Touchstone/Simon and Schuster, 1997), 82.

11. "Walter P. Chrysler Jr. Dies at 79," *New York Times*, September 19, 1988.

12. Russell, "Time Rescues a Collector's Reputation."

13. Teresa Annas, "30 Years Later, Walter Chrysler's Name Cleared in 'Scandal' over Authenticity," *Virginian-Pilot and Ledger-Star*, August 11, 1991.

8. LEAVING PROVINCETOWN

1. Tim Morton, "A Look at Provincetown," *Virginian-Pilot*, January 3, 1971.

2. Gill, "Collector's Puzzling Path."

3. Lipper, "A Search for Self."

4. Patrick O'Higgins, "Art Collector Walter P. Chrysler Jr.," *Town and Country,* December 1977, 140.

5. "Art Collection's Home: Chrysler Disenchanted by Cape's Lack of Support," *Virginian-Pilot,* September 6, 1970.

6. Dorothy Gees Seckler, *Provincetown Painters* (Syracuse, N.Y.: Visual Artist Publications, 1977), 91.

7. Butler, "Patron of the Past."

8. Morton, "A Look at Provincetown."

9. Donald Cantin, "The Revenge of Roger Skillings," *Provincetown Arts* 8 (1992): 137.

9. Finding a New Home

1. Conway B. Thompson, "A Collector Ahead of the Times," *Art Voices/South,* November–December 1980, 10.

2. Ronald A. Kuchta, telephone interview by the author, April 16, 2004

3. Mason, "In Museumland."

4. Lipper, "A Search for Self."

5. John L. "Jack" Gibson, interview by the author, March 11, 2004. Unless otherwise noted, all subsequent quotations by John Gibson are from this interview.

6. In other interviews, the car was approximately the same vintage, but alternately described as a Dodge, a De Soto, and, naturally, a Chrysler.

7. Denzil Skinner, telephone interview by the author, April 15, 2004. Unless otherwise noted, all subsequent quotations by Denzil Skinner are from this interview.

8. Roy Martin, typescript memoir.

9. "Art Collection's Home."

10. Thompson, "A Collector Ahead of the Times."

11. "3 Museum Officials to View Art Gift," *Ledger-Star,* November 11, 1970.

12. "The Chrysler Hassle," editorial, *Ledger-Star,* November 25, 1970.

13. Tim Morton, "Another Chief, 2nd in Year, Quits Museum," *Virginian-Pilot,* December 9, 1970.

14. Tim Morton, "Manager Selected by Norfolk Museum," *Virginian-Pilot,* December 19, 1970.

10. THE CITY REACTS

1. Julie Dalton, interview by the author, May 12, 2004. Unless otherwise noted, all subsequent quotations by Julie Dalton are from this interview.

2. Ibid.

3. Mason, "In Museumland."

4. Walter P. Chrysler Jr. Acceptance speech on receipt of "First Citizen of the Arts" award, October 23. 1980.

11. THE CHRYSLER MUSEUM AT NORFOLK

1. "One to Grow On," editorial, *Virginian-Pilot,* January 11, 1971.

2. Russell, "Time Rescues a Collector's Reputation."

3. Linda Kaufman, interview by the author, January 11, 2004. Unless otherwise noted, all subsequent quotations by Linda Kaufman are from this interview.

4. O'Higgins, "Art Collector Walter P. Chrysler Jr."

5. McGreevy, "Happy Birthday, Walter Chrysler!"

6. Martha Gagliardi, "This Glass Menagerie Valuable Art," *Virginian-Pilot,* June 30, 1971.

7. Kirkland Clarkson, interview by the author, August 20, 2004. Unless otherwise noted, all subsequent quotations by Kirkland Clarkson are from this interview.

8. Rita Marlier, interview by the author, May 30, 2004. Unless otherwise noted, all subsequent quotations by Rita Marlier are from this interview.

12. SETTLING IN

1. John Richardson, *Sacred Monsters, Sacred Masters* (New York: Random House, 2001), 270.

2. Jack Tanzer, interview by the author, March 1, 2004.

3. Malcolm N. Carter, "The Chrysler Museum: Clouded by Controversy," *ARTnews,* February 1976, 57.

4. Eric Zafran, e-mail interview by the author, March 23, 2004.

5. Jack Tanzer, interview by the author, March 1, 2004.

6. Willis Potter, interview by the author, February 4, 2004.

Unless otherwise noted, all subsequent quotations by Willis Potter are from this interview.

7. Bill McAllister, "Art Works Exchanged by Chrysler," *Virginian-Pilot,* October 25, 1972.

8. Ibid.

9. Mason, "In Museumland."

10. Ibid.

11. Tony Cacalano, telephone interview by the author, October 5, 2004.

12. Kenneth Beam, telephone interview by the author, September 15, 2004. Unless otherwise noted, all subsequent quotations by Kenneth Beam are from this interview.

13. Big Changes

1. Ann Vernon, interview by the author, February 23, 2004. Unless otherwise noted, all subsequent quotations by Ann Vernon are from this interview.

2. Don Hunt, "Chrysler Gives Museum $1.4-Million Masterpiece," *Virginian-Pilot,* February 11, 1975.

3. "Museum Acquires Naïve Art," *Virginian-Pilot,* March 30, 1975.

4. Mal Vincent, "Abingdon's Barter: Norfolk Winters for Va. Theater," *Virginian-Pilot,* July 17, 1975.

5. Harry Eagar, "Barter Theater Plan Drawing Mixed Reaction," *Ledger-Star,* May 1, 1975.

6. Tim Morton, "Theater Drops Season, '78 Comeback Planned," *Virginian-Pilot,* August 12, 1976.

7. Cindy Amorese, "Museum Peps Up Monday Nights," *Virginian-Pilot,* July 20, 1975.

8. "The Naked and the Nude," editorial, *Virginian-Pilot,* October 9, 1975.

9. F. D. Cossitt, "Affirms Worth of Man," *Virginian-Pilot,* October 12, 1975.

10. "Chrysler's Youthful Tastes Piqued Parents," *Ledger-Star,* October 27, 1975.

11. Don Hunt, "Chrysler 'Gives' Museum Works It Already Owns," *Virginian-Pilot,* October 29, 1975.

12. Carol Mather, "New Curator Likes the Local Museum Scene," *Virginian-Pilot*, April 25, 1976.

13. Eric Zafran, e-mail interview by the author, March 23, 2004.

14. Connors, "Saga of a Compulsive Collector."

15. F. D. Cossitt, "Quiet Transition Under Way at Chrysler Museum," *Virginian-Pilot*, November 28, 1976.

16. Clifford Hubbard, "Chrysler to Resign 1 Museum Post," *Virginian-Pilot*, November 18, 1976.

17. Jack Tanzer, interview by the author, March 1, 2004.

14. OH! MARIO!

1. "Museum Appointment," *Virginian-Pilot*, December 17, 1976.

2. "Another Museum Crisis," editorial, *Virginian-Pilot*, December 19, 1976.

3. William Ruehlmann, "Amaya Makes Art a Happening," *Ledger-Star*, June 15, 1978.

4. Judith Dressel, telephone interview by the author, August 24, 2004. Unless otherwise noted, all subsequent quotations by Judith Dressel are from this interview.

5. Mike Goodwin, interview by the author, August 25, 2004. Unless otherwise noted, all subsequent quotations by Mike Goodwin are from this interview.

6. Brooks Johnson, interview by the author, March 29, 2004. Unless otherwise noted, all subsequent quotations by Brooks Johnson are from this interview.

7. Ruehlmann, "Amaya Makes Art a Happening."

8. Deby Weyerman, "Museum's Amaya Denies Conflict," *Ledger-Star*, June 2, 1978.

9. Teresa Annas, "Former Chrysler Director Gets His 15 Minutes," *Virginian-Pilot*, July 6, 1996.

10. "Norfolk Honors Walter Chrysler," *Virginian-Pilot*, September 28, 1977.

11. O'Higgins, "Art Collector Walter P. Chrysler Jr."

12. William Ruehlmann, "Art Library Wasting Away," *Ledger-Star*, February 1, 1978.

13. Marvin Leon Lake, "New Chief for Museum," *Virginian-Pilot*, January 23, 1979.

14. "Museum's Director to Step Down," *Virginian-Pilot,* November 21, 1979.

15. "Art Patron Chrysler Honored by Assembly," *Virginian-Pilot,* February 7, 1979.

15. THE LION DECLAWED

1. Tim Morton, "Drifting Chrysler Drops Anchor," *Virginian-Pilot,* July 17, 1980.

2. Ibid.

3. Steadman currently lives in California, where he retired after directing the Toledo (Ohio) Museum. He has since attended seminary and is now an ordained Anglican minister.

16. FAREWELL TO A DEVOTED PARTNER

1. Edythe Harrison, telephone interview by the author, November 22, 2004. Unless otherwise noted, all subsequent quotations by Edythe Harrison are from this interview.

2. Catherine Jordan Wass, interview by the author, January 25, 2004. Unless otherwise noted, all subsequent quotations by Catherine Jordan Wass are from this interview.

3. Irene Roughton, interview by the author, September 15, 2004. Unless otherwise noted, all subsequent quotations by Irene Roughton are from this interview.

4. John Coit, "A Renaissance Woman," *Virginian-Pilot,* January 29, 1982.

17. A DIAMOND JUBILEE

1. "Mr. Chrysler's Museum." *Virginian,* January–February 1985, 75.

2. McGreevy, "Happy Birthday, Mr. Chrysler!"

3. Richard Nilsen, "New Chrysler Donations a Visual Feast," *Virginian-Pilot,* May 18, 1984.

4. Warren Fiske, "Museum Officials Unveil $8-Million Expansion Plan," *Virginian-Pilot,* June 23, 1983.

5. Ibid.

6. Joe Fahy, "Art Appreciation: Curator Hopes to Bring Museum Treasures to More People," *Ledger-Star,* April 18, 1985.

7. "Chrysler Coup: Museum Acquires Sculptures," *Virginian-Pilot and Ledger-Star,* February 28, 1987.

8. Teresa Annas, "Revamped Chrysler Gallery Adds Collection of Mayan Ceramics," *Virginian-Pilot and Ledger-Star,* October 2, 1988.

18. HEIR TO A FORTUNE

1. Arthur Diamonstein, interview by the author, January 19, 2004.Unless otherwise noted, all subsequent quotations by Arthur Diamonstein are from this interview.

2. James B. Oliver, interview by the author, April 4, 2004. Unless otherwise noted, all subsequent quotations by James Oliver are from this interview.

3. Teresa Annas, "The Chrysler Legacy," *Virginian-Pilot and Ledger-Star,* November 6, 1988.

4. Ibid.

5. Jack Chrysler, telephone interview by the author, October 19, 2004. Unless otherwise noted, all subsequent quotations by Jack Chrysler are from this interview.

19. THE AUCTION BLOCK

1. Teresa Annas, "Chrysler Left Art Work to Nephew," *Virginian-Pilot,* October 13, 1988.

2. Teresa Annas, "Chrysler Nephew to Sell Art on Loan to Norfolk Museum," *Virginian-Pilot,* January 12, 1989.

3. Teresa Annas, "Chrysler Masterworks Will Go on Sotheby's Block Thursday, and the World Will Be Watching," *Virginian-Pilot,* May 30, 1989.

4. Teresa Annas, "Chrysler Paintings Set Auction Records," *Virginian-Pilot,* June 2, 1989.

5. Antony Thorncroft, "Saleroom," *Financial Times* (London), June 5, 1989.

6. Teresa Annas, "Sale of Chrysler Works Surpasses Estimates," *Virginian-Pilot,* June 20, 1989.

20. "A PRICELESS BLESSING"

1. Clifford Pearson, "Order out of Chaos," *Architectural Record,* July 1989, 114.

2. Paul Goldberger, "A Museum Exhibits a Splendid Lack of Glitz," *New York Times,* June 4, 1989.

3. Teresa Annas, "Art at Eye Level," *Virginian-Pilot and Ledger-Star,* January 26, 1990.

4. Teresa Annas, "Ex-director Frankel Was Better at Art Than Budgets, Officials Say," *Virginian-Pilot,* April 20, 1996.

5. Bill Hennessey, interview by the author, October 27, 2004. Unless otherwise noted, all subsequent quotations by Bill Hennessey are from this interview.

21. LEGACY

1. Josh Darden, interview by the author, December 22, 2003.

2. Russell, "Time Rescues a Collector's Reputation."

3. Hilton Kramer, "The Chrysler Convertible," *Art and Antiques* (Summer 1989), 125.

4. Evan H. Turner, "Collections, Not Mega-Exhibitions, Make Great Museums," *Virginian-Pilot and Ledger-Star,* February 26, 1989.

5. "Walter P. Chrysler Jr.," editorial, *Virginian-Pilot,* September 20, 1988.

6. Annas, "The Chrysler Legacy."

7. Jim Morrison, "Renovated Chrysler Museum Dedicated," *Ledger-Star,* February 22, 1989.

AFTERWORD

1. "Fulfilling the Legacy of Walter P. Chrysler, Jr.," editorial, *Virginian-Pilot,* October 18, 2002.

2. E-mail message from Bill Hennessey, January 4, 2007.

Sources

Interviews by the Author

Baker, Gary. January 28, 2004.

Beam, Ken. September 15, 2004. Telephone interview.

Busa, Christopher. July 20, 2004.

Cacalano, Tony. October 5, 2004. Telephone interview.

Chandler, Nancy Outland. February 19, 2004.

Chrysler, Jack. October 19, 2004. Telephone interview.

Clark, Mark. February 7, 2004.

Clarkson, Kirkland. August 20, 2004.

Dalton, Julie. May 12, 2004.

Darden, Josh. December 22, 2003.

Diamonstein, Arthur, and Renee Diamonstein. January 19, 2004.

Dressel, Judith. August 24, 2004.

Gibson, John L. "Jack." March 11, 2004.

Goodwin, Mike. August 25, 2004.

Harrison, Edythe. November 22, 2004. Telephone interview.

Harrison, Jefferson C. February 13, 2004.

Hennessey, Bill. October 27, 2004.

Johnson, Brooks. March 29, 2004.

Kashey, Robert. January 12, 2005. Telephone interview.

Kaufman, Linda. January 11, 2004.

Kuchta, Ronald A. April 16, 2004. Telephone interview.

Marlier, Rita. May 30, 2004.

Merrill, Nancy. January 3, 2004.

Nichols, Dr. Marguerite. June 10, 2004.

Oliver, James B. April 4, 2004.

Outland, Grover. February 25, 2004.

Potter, Willis. February 4, 2004.

Rosenblatt, Minna. February 29, 2004.

Roughton, Irene. September 15, 2004.

Skinner, Denzil. April 15, 2004. Telephone interview.

Smith, Louise Outland. April 25, 2004.

Sokolowski, Tom. March 19, 2004.

Steadman, David. March 31, 2004. Telephone interview.

Tanzer, Jack. March 1, 2004; and telephone interview on January 12, 2005.

Vernon, Ann. February 23, 2004.

Wass, Catherine Jordan. January 25, 2004.

Werth, Matthew. May 27, 2004.

Zafran, Eric. March 23, 2004. E-mail interview.

OTHER SOURCES

Amorese, Cindy. "Museum Peps Up Monday Nights." *Virginian-Pilot,* July 20, 1975.

Andelman, David A. "Fake-Art Seller in Chrysler Case Accused Again: Gallery Trying to Recover $1 Million for 23 Works." *New York Times,* December 7, 1979.

Annas, Teresa. "Art at Eye Level: For New Museum Director Robert H. Frankel, Serving the Chrysler Means Moving up, and Reaching Out." *Virginian-Pilot and Ledger-Star,* January 26 1990.

———. "Chrysler Left Art Work to Nephew: Most of Family Trust Fund to Go to the Museum." *Virginian-Pilot,* October 13, 1988.

———. "The Chrysler Legacy: With a Healthy Bequest and February Reopening, the Museum Sets Course without Its Benefactor." *Virginian-Pilot and Ledger-Star,* November 6, 1988.

———. "Chrysler Masterworks Will Go on Sotheby's Block Thursday, and the World Will be Watching." *Virginian-Pilot,* May 30, 1989.

———. "Chrysler Museum Director Frankel Quits His Post: After

Six Years in the Norfolk Job, He Will Run a Smaller Museum in California." *Virginian-Pilot,* October 17, 1995.

————. "Chrysler Nephew to Sell Art on Loan to Norfolk Museum." *Virginian-Pilot,* January 12, 1989.

————. "Chrysler Paintings Set Auction Records: 121 of Works Inherited by Nephew Fetch $18.5 Million in New York." *Virginian-Pilot,* June 2, 1989.

————. "Ex-Director Frankel Was Better at Art Than Budgets, Officials Say." *Virginian-Pilot,* April 20, 1996.

————. "Facing Debts, Chrysler Museum Depleted Rainy-Day Fund." *Virginian-Pilot,* April 20, 1996.

————. "Former Chrysler Director Gets His 15 Minutes." *Virginian-Pilot,* July 6, 1996.

————. "Man of Ideas Left His Mark on Museum 3 Decades Ago: Director of the Chrysler's Forerunner in 1960s Has Died at 81." *Virginian-Pilot,* August 12, 1999.

————. "Revamped Chrysler Gallery Adds Collection of Mayan Ceramics." *Virginian-Pilot and Ledger-Star,* October 2, 1988.

————. "Sale of Chrysler Works Surpasses Estimates." *Virginian-Pilot,* June 20, 1989.

————. "30 Years Later, Walter Chrysler's Name Cleared in 'Scandal' over Authenticity." *Virginian-Pilot and Ledger-Star,* August 11, 1991.

————. "$2 Million Pledged to Museum." *Virginian-Pilot,* December 22, 1983.

"Another Museum Crisis." Editorial. *Virginian-Pilot,* December 19, 1976.

"Another Professional Job Ended at Art Museum." *Ledger-Star,* July 31, 1971.

"Art Collection's Home: Chrysler Disenchanted by Cape's Lack of Support." *Virginian-Pilot,* September 6, 1970.

"Art Paper at Dartmouth." *New York Times,* May 9, 1930.

"Art Patron Chrysler Honored by Assembly." *Virginian-Pilot,* February 7, 1979.

"Art Patroness Succumbs." *Mecklenburg Sun,* January 28, 1982.

"Art Society Votes: Chrysler Gift Cleared." *Virginian-Pilot.* April 3, 1971.

"Arts Society Board for Chrysler Gift." *Virginian-Pilot,* February 26, 1971.

Barr, Margaret Scolari. "Our Campaigns." *New Criterion* (Summer 1987): 23–74.

Bayer, Richard C. "Chrysler Appointment Conciliatory Move." *Ledger-Star,* November 28, 1972.

Berkman, Florence. "Chrysler's Museum Houses Art Collection Begun at 14." *Hartford Times,* August 29, 1959.

"The Biggest Museum Gap." Editorial. *Ledger-Star,* July 8, 1967.

Blazevig, R. L. Letter to the author. December 22, 2004.

Brockett, Omeda. "Chrysler Art Collections Enjoyed by Many: Mrs. Chrysler Visits Parents in Norfolk. *Virginian-Pilot and Portsmouth Star,* April 8, 1956.

Butler, Mary Ellen. "Patron of the Past: Chrysler Brought Glamour and Great Masters, Then Departed Abruptly." *Provincetown Banner,* July 1, 1999.

Cantin, Donald. "The Revenge of Roger Skillings." *Provincetown Arts* 8 (1992): 137.

Carter, Malcolm N. "The Chrysler Museum: Clouded by Controversy." *ARTnews,* February 1976.

Christison, Muriel B. "The Chrysler Story." Typescript, ca. 1946. Standing files, Jean Outland Chrysler Art Library.

"The Chrysler Affair." *Newsweek,* November 26, 1962, 90.

"Chrysler Appointed to Museum Board." *Virginian-Pilot,* January 22, 1969.

"Chrysler Art on View." *New York Times,* February 2, 1941.

"Chrysler Building." New York History. http://www.newyorkhistory .info/42nd-Street/chryslerbuilding.html.

"Chrysler Buys Old Club: Historic Virginia Place, Taken by Racing Man for $175,000." *New York Times,* May 6, 1941.

"Chrysler Coup: Museum Acquires Sculptures." *Virginian-Pilot and Ledger-Star,* February 28, 1987.

"Chrysler Gift: Dispute May Go to Court." *Virginian-Pilot,* January 20, 1971.

"The Chrysler Hassle." Editorial. *Ledger-Star,* November 25, 1970.

"Chrysler Opens New Gallery." *New York Times,* March 8, 1932.

"Chrysler Speeds by Special Train to Hanover to Side of Son, Operated upon at Dartmouth." *New York Times,* November 10, 1930.

SOURCES

"The Chrysler Treasure." Editorial. *Virginian-Pilot,* March 30, 1983.

Chrysler, Walter P., in collaboration with Boyden Sparkes. *Life of an American Workman.* New York: Saturday Evening Post/Curtis, 1937.

Chrysler, Walter P., Jr. Acceptance speech on receipt of "First Citizen of the Arts" Award from the Metropolitan Arts Congress, Norfolk, Va. October 23, 1980.

"A Chrysler Weds a Sykes." *Life,* May 9, 1938, 58.

"Chrysler's Collection—His Credo." *Art Digest,* October 1, 1937, 11, 22.

"The Chrysler's Leadership." Editorial. *Virginian-Pilot and Ledger Star,* April 14, 1985.

"Chrysler's Love of Art Will Keep His Memory Alive, Minister Says." *Ledger-Star,* September 21, 1988.

"Chrysler's Youthful Tastes Piqued Parents." *Ledger-Star,* October 27, 1975.

Coit, John. "A Renaissance Woman." *Virginian-Pilot,* January 29, 1982.

Coleman, Sharon. "The Hidden Treasures of Jean Chrysler." *Norfolk Compass,* July 26, 1981.

Connors, Thomas. "Saga of a Compulsive Collector." *M,* June 1989, 4–6.

Cossitt, F. D. "Affirms Worth of Man." *Virginian-Pilot,* October 12, 1975.

———. "The Chrysler Shows Works of Indiana." *Virginian-Pilot,* December 2, 1977.

———. "Norfolk Museum at the Crossroads." *Virginian-Pilot,* October 8, 1967.

———. "Quiet Transition Under Way at Chrysler Museum." *Virginian-Pilot,* November 28, 1976.

———. "A Silencer for Those Who Criticized." *Virginian-Pilot,* April 12, 1972.

Coureas, Loretta. "Benefactors Bask in Museum's New Glow." *Ledger-Star,* November 29, 1967.

Curcio, Vincent. *Chrysler: The Life and Times of an Automotive Genius.* New York: Oxford University Press, 2000.

"Deputy Director Named at Chrysler Museum." *Norfolk Compass,* November 15, 1984.

"Dispute May Go to Court" *Virginian-Pilot,* January 20, 1971.

Eagar, Harry. "Barter Theater Plan Drawing Mixed Reaction." *Ledger-Star,* May 1, 1975.

Fahy, Joe. "Art Appreciation: Curator Hopes to Bring Museum Treasures to More People." *Ledger-Star,* April 18, 1985.

———. "Chrysler Produces Study Guide on Art That Excites Educators." *Virginian-Pilot and Ledger-Star,* December 22, 1985.

———. "More Than Space Is at Stake in Chrysler Expansion." *Virginian-Pilot and Ledger-Star,* August 4, 1985.

"Fakes and Forgeries." Art Dealers Association Web site, www .artdealers.org/.

Fiske, Warren. "Museum Officials Unveil $8-Million Expansion Plan." *Virginian-Pilot,* June 23, 1983.

"A Florentine Palace and a Princely Gift." Editorial. *Virginian-Pilot,* September 23, 1960.

Forgey, Benjamin. "The Chrysler Museum, Suddenly Splendid: A Muddled Eyesore Transformed into a Handsome Asset in Norfolk." *Washington Post,* February 26, 1989.

"Forum: What Motivates a Person to Be a Collector of Art?" *American Artist,* November 1980.

Friddell, Guy. "Ark and Art." *Virginian-Pilot,* March 27, 1969.

Gagliardi, Martha. "This Glass Menagerie Valuable Art." *Virginian-Pilot,* June 30, 1971.

Gardner, Ralph D. "Walter Chrysler's Favorite Museum." *Collector Editions* 6. no. 2 (Spring 1978): 22.

"Gift Expands Art Library at Chrysler." *Virginian-Pilot,* January 6, 1978.

Gill, William J. "The Collector's Puzzling Path." *Life,* November 2, 1962.

———. "Strange Story of Walter Chrysler Jr. and the Great Art Scandal," *Life,* November 2, 1962, 91–94.

Goldberger, Paul. "A Museum Exhibits a Splendid Lack of Glitz." *New York Times,* June 4, 1989.

Hemphill, Chris. "Walter P. Chrysler Jr.: How I Made 1.6 Million from a $450 Picasso." *Interview,* June 1978.

Hoelterhoff, Manuela. "How a Southern City Became an Art Center." *Wall Street Journal,* April 1, 1976.

Hofheimer, Jo Ann Mervis. *Annie Wood, a Portrait: The Life and Times of the Founder of the Irene Leache Memorial.* Norfolk: Irene Leache Memorial, 1996.

Hoving, Thomas. *False Impressions: The Hunt for Big-Time Art Fakes.* New York: Touchstone/Simon and Schuster: 1997.

Hubbard, Clifford. "Chrysler to Resign 1 Museum Post." *Virginian-Pilot,* November 18, 1976.

————. "Fire Inflicts Heavy Damage to Historic Selden House." *Virginian-Pilot,* April 7, 1973.

Hunt, Don. "Chrysler Gives Museum $1.4-Million Masterpiece." *Virginian-Pilot,* February 11, 1975.

————. "Chrysler 'Gives' Museum Works It Already Owns." *Virginian-Pilot,* October 29, 1975.

"Jean Chrysler, 60, Dies." *Virginian-Pilot,* January 27, 1982.

Justice, Cornelia. "Chrysler Discusses Plans for Norfolk." *Ledger-Star,* September 5, 1970.

————. "New Curator Joins Chrysler from N.Y." *Ledger-Star,* March 26, 1976.

————. "New Museum Director Knows Way Around." *Ledger-Star,* January 7, 1977.

Keel, Ronnie. "Apollo Exhibit Opens Tonight: Tennis-Ball-Sized Moon Rock in Chrysler Museum Display." *Ledger-Star,* August 28, 1971.

Kramer, Hilton. "The Chrysler Convertible: A Happy Ending to What Looked Like a Cliffhanger." *Art and Antiques* 6 (Summer 1989): 125.

Kuchta, Ronald A. "The Chrysler Art Museum." Typescript. Jean Outland Chrysler Library archives. October 15, 1966.

————. "Homage to Walter Chrysler: The Provincetown Years." Essay included on an invitation to an exhibit at the Katzen-Brown Gallery. January 1989.

Lake, Marvin Leon. "Chrysler's Director to Take Leave." *Virginian-Pilot,* June 2, 1978.

————. "Museum to Cut Hours to 32 a Week." *Virginian-Pilot,* September 17, 1977.

————. "New Chief for Museum." *Virginian-Pilot,* January 23, 1979.

Lerch, John. "Walter P. Chrysler Jr.'s Collection of Twentieth-Century Masterpieces." *Country Life,* May 1938, 44–47.

Lipper, Bob. "A Search for Self, A Stab at Immortality." *Virginian-Pilot,* July 3, 1977.

Manso, Peter. *Ptown: Art, Sex, and Money on the Outer Cape.* New York: Scribner, 2002.

"Marguerite Chrysler Awarded Reno Decree." *Reno Evening Gazette,* December 5, 1939.

"Marguerite Sykes Has Church Bridal: Chapel of St. Bartholomew's Scene of Her Marriage to Walter P. Chrysler Jr." *New York Times,* April 30, 1938.

Martin, Roy. Typescript memoir. Quoted with the permission of Mrs. Louise Martin.

Mason, Robert. "In Museumland." Typescript. Quoted with the permission of Fran Mason Irvin.

Mather, Carol. "New Curator Likes the Local Museum Scene." *Virginian-Pilot,* April 25 1976.

McAllister, Bill. "Art Works Exchanged by Chrysler." *Virginian-Pilot,* October 25, 1972.

———. "Chrysler Plans Rembrandt Gift." *Virginian-Pilot,* December 20, 1972.

McGreevy, Linda. "Happy Birthday Walter Chrysler! On His 75th Birthday, the Man Behind the Museum Bestows a Wonderful Gift on Us—10 Major Works of Art." *Port Folio* 2, no. 4 (May 22–28, 1984): 5–6.

"Membership of Museum Integrated." *Ledger-Dispatch,* May 12, 1964.

"Miss Jean Outland Bride of Walter P. Chrysler Jr., at Freemason Street Church." *Virginian-Pilot,* January 14, 1945.

Morrison, Jim. "Renovated Chrysler Museum Dedicated." *Ledger-Star,* February 22, 1989.

Morton, Tim. "Another Chief, 2nd in Year, Quits Museum." *Virginian-Pilot,* December 9, 1970.

———. "Chrysler Art Acceptance Urged." *Virginian-Pilot,* January 20, 1971.

———. "Chrysler Art Accepted, 5 to 4." *Virginian-Pilot,* February 9, 1971.

———. "Drifting Chrysler Drops Anchor: Museum to Name New Leadership." *Virginian-Pilot,* July 17, 1980.

———. "A Look at Provincetown." *Virginian-Pilot,* January 3, 1971.

———. "Manager Selected by Norfolk Museum." *Virginian-Pilot,* December 19, 1970.

———. "Museum Animals Go Free." *Virginian-Pilot,* July 20, 1969.

———. "Museum Gets $45,000 in 'Challenge' Grant." *Virginian-Pilot,* October 20, 1978.

———. "Theater Drops Season, '78 Comeback Planned." *Virginian-Pilot,* August 12, 1976.

"Mr. Chrysler's Museum." *Virginian* 7, no. 1 (Winter/January–February 1985): 75–79.

"Museum Acquires Naïve Art." *Virginian-Pilot,* March 30, 1975.

"Museum Appointment." *Virginian-Pilot,* December 17, 1976.

"Museum Asks $1 Donation." *Virginian-Pilot,* April 3, 1977.

"Museum Funds Held Back." *Virginian-Pilot,* July 24, 1968.

"Museum Names Amaya Director." *Virginian-Pilot,* March 2, 1977.

"Museum's Curator to Leave Soon." *Virginian-Pilot,* March 26, 1976.

"Museum's Director to Step Down." *Virginian-Pilot,* November 21, 1979.

"Music of All Periods: A Listening Room Installed at Museum." *Virginian-Pilot,* June 7, 1975.

"The Naked and the Nude." Editorial. *Virginian-Pilot,* October 9, 1975.

"New Chrysler Gift in Modern Museum: Manufacturer's Son Donates Collection of Surrealist Books and Material." *New York Times,* November 29, 1936.

Nilsen, Richard. "New Chrysler Donations a Visual Feast." *Virginian-Pilot,* May 18, 1984.

"Norfolk Honors Walter Chrysler." *Virginian-Pilot,* September 28, 1977.

"Norfolk Museum of Arts and Sciences Is Reality; Opens with Exhibit Today." *Virginian-Pilot,* March 5, 1933.

O'Higgins, Patrick. "Art Collector Walter P. Chrysler Jr.: His Connoisseurship Has Demonstrated That Collecting Itself, Indeed, Can Be an Art. *Town and Country,* December 1977, 140.

"One to Grow On." Editorial. *Virginian-Pilot,* January 11, 1971.

Pearson, Clifford. "Order out of Chaos." *Architectural Record,* July 1989, 114.

Perlmutter, Jack. "Walter P. Chrysler Jr.: 'A Collector Can Never be Bored.'" *Art Voices/South* 1, no. 1 (July–August 1978): 6.

Reif, Rita. "A Master Sale: One of the Weightiest Auctions of Art in Decades." *Chicago Tribune,* January 22, 1989.

Richardson, John. *Sacred Monsters, Sacred Masters.* New York: Random House, 2001.

Rohrer, Bert. "Museum Wing Opens to over 4,000." *Virginian-Pilot,* March 1, 1976.

Ruehlmann, William. "Amaya Makes Art a Happening: A Lavish Controversial Showman." *Ledger-Star,* June 15, 1978.

———. "Art Library Wasting Away: Million-Dollar Collection and No Place to Put It." *Ledger-Star,* February 1, 1978.

———. "Man Behind the Museum." *Virginian-Pilot and Ledger-Star,* October 19, 1980.

Russell, John. "Time Rescues a Collector's Reputation." *New York Times,* August 11, 1991.

"Scent of Scandal." *Time,* October 26, 1962.

Seckler, Dorothy Gees. *Provincetown Painters: 1890's–1970's.* Syracuse, N.Y.: Visual Artist Publications, 1977, 89–92. Published for an exhibition organized by Ronald A. Kuchta and held April 1– June 6, 1977, at the Everson Museum of Art of Syracuse and Onondaga County, Syracuse, New York, and the Provincetown Art Association, August 15–September 5, 1977.

Sessa, Cammy. "An Eventful Visit Home for Jean Chrysler." *Virginian-Pilot,* November 30, 1967.

"Society's Most-Sought Girl Won by Heir." *Ironwood (Mich.) Daily Globe,* February 7, 1938.

Steadman, Ethel A. "Lawsuit at Museum Fails." *Virginian-Pilot,* December 21, 1972.

Stevens, William K. "Museum Takes Giant Step: Benefactor and City Council Make $1.2 Million Expansion Possible." *Virginian-Pilot,* February 23, 1964.

Stone, Steve, and Guy Friddell. "Chrysler's Love of Life Leaves a Gift for All: Art Collector Is Remembered for Generosity, Taste, Foresight." *Virginian-Pilot,* September 19, 1988.

Swift, Earl, and Teresa Annas. "Museum Missed Chrysler Treasure by Hours: Benefactor Died Less Than 2 Days before Meeting to Sign New Will. *Virginian-Pilot and Ledger-Star,* April 9, 1989.

Taylor, Maureen. "Woman Behind the Man: Being Mrs. Walter P. Chrysler Jr. Is 'Fun.' " *Ledger-Star,* November 29, 1967.

Tazewell, William L. "Chrysler Museum Mounts Picasso Art: 20 Works Included in Showing." *Virginian-Pilot,* June 10, 1973.

———. "A Growing Museum in Transition." *Virginian-Pilot,* September 1, 1963.

"Temperature Corp." *Time,* July 23, 1934.

"Theatre Arts Spotlights: Walter P. Chrysler Jr." *Theatre Arts* 36, no. 9 (September 1952): 21.

Thompson, Conway B. "A Collector Ahead of the Times: Walter P. Chrysler Jr. Candidly Reminisces about His Early Life, and Discusses his Diverse Art Collection Which Spawned the Chrysler Museum in Norfolk, Virginia." *Art Voices/South,* November–December 1980, 10–11.

Thorncroft, Antony. "Saleroom." *Financial Times* (London), June 5, 1989.

"3 Museum Officials to View Art Gift." *Ledger Star,* November 11, 1970.

Tucker, George Holbert. "Museum Gets Italian Art: Chrysler Collection to Launch New Wing." *Virginian-Pilot,* May 21, 1967.

———. "Museum Wing Dedicated." *Virginian-Pilot,* December 3, 1967.

Vincent, Mal. "Abingdon's Barter: Norfolk Winters for Va. Theater." *Virginian-Pilot,* July 17, 1975.

"Wahlig to Retire from Museum Job." *Virginian-Pilot,* July 31, 1976.

"Walter Chrysler Dies at 79: Built up Museum, Art Collection." *Virginian-Pilot and Ledger-Star,* September 18, 1988.

"Walter P. Chrysler Jr. Dies at 79." *New York Times,* September 19, 1988.

"Walter Chrysler Jr. to Be a Publisher: Auto Man Will Serve under Son on Board of New Concern—12 Classics to Be Printed." *New York Times,* September 10, 1930.

"Walter H. Sykes Jr., Broker, Dead at 58: Former Head of the Association of Stock Exchange Firms Was Graduate of Yale." *New York Times,* September 29, 1936.

187

"Walter P. Chrysler." Editorial. *New York Times,* August 20, 1940.

"Walter P. Chrysler Jr." *Virginian-Pilot,* September 20, 1988.

"Walter P. Chrysler Jr. Quits Navy." *New York Times,* December 16, 1944.

"Warehouse Art." Talk of the Town column. *New Yorker,* December 29, 1956, 15–16.

Weyerman, Deby. "Museum's Amaya Denies Conflict." *Ledger-Star,* June 2, 1978.

Willard, Charlotte. "Walter P. Chrysler, Jr., Exhibits His Personal History of Art." *Look,* March 6, 1956, 44.

Wojtowicz, Robert, Ph.D. Unpublished biographical research on Walter P. Chrysler Jr., 2004.

Wood, William H. "Chrysler Giving Valuable Paintings." *Ledger-Star,* October 28, 1975.

Young, Sharon. "Chrysler Museum to Open Gallery in Former City Hall on Monday." *Norfolk Compass,* December 2, 1984.

INDEX